BUILDING BRANDS IN A SUDDENLY CHANGED WORLD

A HANDBOOK OF THE MADDENING SHIFTS THAT TURNED THINGS UP SIDE DOWN THIS DECADE ALONE, WHAT'S NEXT AND WHAT IT ALL MEANS FOR BUSINESS AND BRANDS.

POOJA NAIR

For my Achan, Amma, and Ammuma for instilling the habit of keen observation in me right from when I was a little child. Not just observing, but also curiosity about why and how, guiding me in exploration and discovery. And for my brother, who continues to orient me into thinking laterally just by being who he is.

Contents

Contents

Preface

I started this project nine months ago with the goal of maintaining a ready reckoner of current realities that I should not lose sight of when working on brand strategy. The current landscape warrants an overhaul of how we approach brand building, both online and offline. The endeavour unraveled a host of insights and knowledge, which I meticulously researched and documented. This also helped me develop an informed vision of things to come.

Change is not new to us. The idea of taking the unexpected into account is implicit in any good strategy. However, the rate and vastness of change today have put us in Tom's plight in that episode of Tom and Jerry when he gets caught under a just-hit and slightly tilted bookshelf. The hardcover at the very edge succumbs to gravity and lands straight on Tom's head. He barely recovers from the shock of the hit when the next book lands in the same spot. Then the shelf tilts further due to the growing imbalance of weight, making more books slide and land on Tom's head faster each time. Tom barely gets a chance to move away from under the cascade, as book after book hits him on the head. Most of us are seeing stars in daylight, collapsing under the merciless frequency of reality checks.

This book attempts to serve as an essential handbook for these maddening shifts that have impacted consumer culture, behaviour, business approaches, marketing, and advertising in the last decade alone—and will most likely shape the world in the times to come. As a bonus, it opens up ideas and opportunities for the brands you work on, the business you run, or the one you might just decide to start yourself.

Acknowledgements

I am grateful to Meraj Hasan for being the first person to make me see that I had what it takes to be an effective brand strategist. His words, *"Think of it as if it were your own business,"* drive my conviction in my work as a brand strategist to this day.

Prabhakar Mundkur, for showing me that it is possible to stay trendier than most young people, no matter your age. He encouraged me to make a presentation on Scenario Planning way back in 2006—an orientation of thought that has shaped me as a strategist. What many don't know about him is that he is a rockstar. Literally. He is a singer, guitarist, and keyboardist and was part of one of the hottest bands in India in the '60s: The Savages. Prabs showed me, in my early career, that creative people make the best strategists. I have never held myself back from my creative pursuits while being a brand strategist, thanks to Prabs.

Subramanyeswar S, for being a rock of a leader and mentor from the day he first interviewed me for a job opening at Saatchi & Saatchi for their Colombo, Sri Lanka office. His undeterred demonstration of faith in my capabilities as a professional and as a human being is something that has kept me going during hostile and challenging situations I have had to face at the hands of others in the same industry. Solid leaders are extremely rare to come by, and I can't believe my luck that one of them is my friend.

Prem Narayan, for placing his full trust in me to handle important clients at Ogilvy India out of their Mumbai office. He told me, *"I want your clients to never ask for Prem."* I loved the simplicity of the mandate, and I'd like to think

I delivered. I will never be able to express how thankful I am to Prem for accommodating my need to take a month off at a stretch when I landed the opportunity to act in the Akshay Kumar starrer Bollywood film (Airlift, 2015) while being employed at Ogilvy. As a leader, that was a call he took, and this is only one of the things I admire him deeply for. The experience, of course, enriched my acumen as a creative industry professional.

Joseph George, who decided not to hire me after hours of conversations in July 2020. The gem of a person that he is, he ensured I did not feel less worthy by giving me something better instead. He told me to write more. Not just that, he showed me he meant it by introducing me to Raahil Chopra, Managing Editor of Campaign India, who graciously published several of my write-ups since then. Joe had written to Raahil, "...*her absolutely delightful professional journey so far has made her a natural at writing on brands, consumers, and culture.*" The lasting impression these words had on me is more than evident. Thank you, Joe, from the bottom of my heart.

Prof. David Rogers, faculty member, Columbia Business School, for opening my eyes to the compelling and immediate need to transform ourselves and our businesses for the digital age. What I learned doing his program on digital marketing strategies is the one course that readied me to build strategies for a rapidly changing marketplace. The ideas in this book are deeply influenced by what I learned from him in the last three years.

Lastly, but also mostly, Amith Prabhu, for being the sparkler of ideas that he is. He said to me two years ago, "*Write a piece a week for Reputation Today (his magazine), and when you have 30 stories, you can turn it into a book.*" The way he put it made it sound simple and doable. Nine months ago, I acted on this idea, and the result is this book. I can't thank you enough, Amith.

I urge you to Google and follow all seven people thanked here to learn about some true gems—not just as business strategists, but as leaders and as people.

WHY THIS BOOK

CHAPTER I

Tackling Resistance To Change

Fountain pens were a helpful innovation after feather tips that needed to be repeatedly dipped in a bottle of ink. It is safe to guess that people who had spent their entire careers using the feather tip may have hated it anyway. Automatic gears are an innovation in automobiles, making driving smoother. It is not uncommon to come across driving enthusiasts who feel unenthusiastic about this shift in gears, to do away with gears altogether. Digital cameras were an innovation in photography, freeing snappers (that's what we called them before Snapchat) from the need to be careful with film rolls and waiting for at least 24 hours for them to develop to see how the capture turned out. Older professional photographers possibly continue to lament how photography as an art form has been compromised. The challenges this change posed to Eastman Kodak Company, or simply Kodak, a leading name in this domain since the 1880s, serves as an important lesson.

If we see history as a guide, we will see the importance of developing a vision of things to come. Kodak entered the printer ink business, which also faced a decline as we started to shift away from printouts to online copies. Innovations can topple companies, unless they transform themselves for the future instead of reacting to challenges as and when it becomes impossible to look away. Transformations are not easy, but as a first step, we need to tackle the subconscious or conscious resistance to change.

Change makes us uneasy. Not just in technology but also in value systems and the status quo. Heraclitus, the Greek philosopher, famously noted that change is the only constant in life. Surely, he was talking about gradual change, considering that he was from ancient times. What he could not have envisioned then was that this constant change was also going to increase at an exponential rate a few centuries down the line. Good for him. Even imagining it could have given anyone living in those times a stroke.

Cut to today: it doesn't matter how we feel about all this non-gradual change. What matters is that we accept its inevitability. To heighten our chances of not sinking in a quicksand of irrelevance, we need to inculcate the ability to surf the waves of change and avoid crashing against them with ridicule and derision.

If it's any solace, change, if approached right, can be good for business and the self. It improves productivity and growth. It often spells the fixing of something that has been begging to be fixed. It can only be useful to **see** change and understand it.

That brings me to the three kinds of responses to the idea of 'things are changing' that I have witnessed amongst leaders at the organizations I have been employed at over the past two decades:

Head in the sand – refusal to acknowledge the impending pandemic or tsunami of change.

Techno-paranoia – the first-ever episode of the Netflix series Black Mirror, released in 2011, is a good example. It was based on the premise that, in the near future, the entire human race would turn collectively voyeuristic, almost in synchronized harmony. That near future has come and gone. What is depicted in that very popular episode remains far-fetched. The popularity of that show, especially in the 2010s, is testimony to the fact that its sentiments echoed the irrational thought process in people's minds.

Seeing opportunity – analyzing developments, watching trends in real time, introspecting on personal prejudices and fears, evaluating, and ideating on how to make the most of the change.

Needless to say, there are heavy costs and risks involved in keeping denial as your first line of defense. At the other extreme, believing that technology is out to end our careers and the human species itself will simply stun us into knee-jerk reactions. These extremes also happen to be the most widely seen responses.

"The ones who rise above stay ahead."

Organizations and individuals who develop an openness to shed a major chunk of all that they have ever learned tend to stay ahead. It requires us, especially in positions of seniority, to let go of our ego and get out of our comfort zones where we are the most knowledgeable and experienced. It takes immense humility to stay new-minded and relevant.

As the value of the currency in which we are millionaires today fades, it is possible for us to keep earning in a new currency. This book is intended to accompany you on this train of thought. Putting it together has helped me see and embrace change. I hope it does the same for you.

Resistance To Change

PEOPLE HAVE SUDDENLY CHANGED

CHAPTER II

Fluidity Of Existence

When Facebook validated 'it's complicated' as a relationship status in the mid-2000s, it was an amusing novelty for many. Many nodded in approval as they felt the relief of no longer having to limit themselves to the binary of single/committed. Today, 20 years later, this breakdown of rigidity is apparent in other areas – work culture, gender identity, beauty standards, and age-related notions, to name a few.

The lack of fixed templates can be unsettling. Every generation before Gen Z was attuned to being forced into boxes. Success for us relied on how well we could cope with being boxed. But today, that is no longer required, making way for a generation that rejects templates. Not that people from previous generations don't have the same facility, just that they prefer accusing Gen Z of entitlement instead. What we need to see is that Gen Z and people with Gen Z mindsets are simply making the most of the opportunities available to all of us today. There is no reason for anyone not to.

Lamenting about how everything is changing has always been a waste of time. Greek Philosopher Heraclitus pointed it out before 475 BC (the recorded year of his death). "The only thing that is constant is change," he is known to have observed. Acknowledging this ancient wisdom pushes us to be on our toes. We need to rewire ourselves to succeed in a world where little is fixed. We are all coping with change, but those with a Gen Z mindset are busy flipping this impermanence and fluidity of everything to make things better for themselves—in careers, in relationships, and in society by large.

A more open, accepting youth is growing older, accustomed to facing vulnerabilities and likewise assured of their strengths. They drive open conversations about toxicity in relationships and workplaces, about mental well-being alongside physical well-being, about fixed definitions of genders and age groups, and about the futility of judgments based on stereotypes.

It is a mere *transfer of entitlement* from those considered to be in power onto the hands of the people. We are realizing that there are many other opportunities out there for us to find the right fit for ourselves. We also have the convenience of making things ourselves or starting something on our own using near-zero capital. So far, people accepted the tyranny of corporate ladder-climbing or sheer corporate surviving because we had no way out.

"Now there is a way out of notions and situations that threaten our sense of self-worth."

Three years ago, I witnessed a consumer research for a South Indian beauty brand where young respondents from tier 2 and 3 cities in India answered, *"me"* quite matter-of-factly to the question, *"Who is the most beautiful woman in the world, according to you?"*. This was the first time in my career spanning 20 years during which I have attended countless consumer research sessions while working for Nivea, Schwarzkopf, Garnier, Pond's Beauty, and Tresemmé with the corresponding ad agencies on record. The easy self-confidence in these girls made me teary-eyed. The research moderator was baffled every time she got this answer. Her following question, dictated by the ad agency I worked at—*"What (physical) features make her so beautiful according to you?"*—had lost relevance. But is this reality being conveyed to the masters of brand strategy on their toxically overworked revolving chairs? I don't know because I was disallowed from using the DG (Discussion Guide) I had put together for this research and advised to use the 'time-tested' one instead. I am guilty of being too exhausted to argue by then. How many heads at legacy ad agencies are appointed based on their ability to adapt to the change in thought and action the times call for? Mostly, too little, too late. Leaving adequate time and need-gaps for indie brands to silently rise and shine with their new-age, in-house brand marketing teams.

If we pay attention, we will **see** evidence of this embrace of fluidity all around us. A year ago, in 2023, at a health clinic called 'Proactive for Her,' I was asked by a lady filling out the form with preliminary health information about me, *"You identify as...?"* It took me a moment to understand the question and another moment to think about how I was supposed to answer it. I blurted out unsurely, *"her?...she?"*. She got her information. Patient is an old millennial. She confirmed it by asking me my age for the form. I'll admit this was at a state-of-the-art clinic in Bangalore, one of the top metros in India, but still, this clinic that advertises itself as 'LGBTQA affirmative' with seven physical branches across the city and a digital presence across the country is representative of the trajectory in which consumer expectations are moving. We now have a clinic that cares for wealthy LGBTQA folks. It's a start.

Templates are being replaced by what I call fluidplates. Fluidplates are where individuals can explore and express while constantly reinventing themselves. Shifting careers, hairdos, sexuality, pace of life and addresses until they settle on what they identify with most, no matter how long it takes and how many back-and-forth shifts it takes.

Brands need to amend their brand templates for fluidplates too. Tough nut to crack, no doubt, but that's the nut that needs cracking. We need to ensure we don't push ourselves into an irrelevant corner by taking care to be inclusive, pro-choice, pro-experimentation, and pro-freedom

Fluidity Of Existence

CHAPTER III

No 'Boss'

The sudden acceleration of process innovation and digitization is making companies around the globe scramble to adjust. Among other things, this has increased the expectations from leadership. In simpler times, when all was set in fixed formats, all good leadership entailed was being on top of the hierarchy, projecting authority, and making decisions with or without consulting the team. A good leader essentially was a 'boss' with some charisma thrown in for good measure. Your team feared and depended on you. Today, good leadership has turned into something entirely different.

I wonder how many people in leadership positions within organizations have cared to study leadership. This curiosity stems from what I have and continue to see at various communications agencies, from my conversations with people employed in the IT sector and the entertainment sector, and from the recent news about EY India's response to the death of Anna Sebastian Perayil, allegedly due to being overloaded with work. It is worth noting that this is a case of an ambitious, hardworking Gen Z fresher dying at the hands of an employer who felt *entitled* to mercilessly overload her with work. What message does this send out to the living Gen Z?

It makes me wonder, based on what do team leaders, heads of departments, and higher officials measure themselves as being good or bad as leaders? Or is the style not considered as important for the P&L (Profit and Loss) of the company? I myself never thought of googling leadership when I was in leadership roles. But I did now. For this book. I hope you and your team benefit from it.

I am guessing that people who feel super productive after a day of bossing everyone around at work would find it fascinating that there are indeed three kinds of academically recognized leadership styles, each with its own pros and cons:

The Autocratic Leader – resented but takes charge.

The Democratic Leader – cultivates a team of motivated, efficient, and confident talent. May not be feared but is deeply respected.

The Laissez-Faire Style – lets the team operate without interference. Comes with the risk of a loss of shared vision and growth.

Recent developments in the consumer and business landscape have led to renewed focus on a fourth kind of leadership. It happens to be the exact opposite of the 'boss style,' the only style most of us know about. It's called 'servant leadership.' When I first heard of it, I remember thinking, 'Wow! Now, I have seen (read) everything.' But the more I read about it, the more I see why it makes complete sense.

The idea of 'Servant Leadership' actually dates to the 1970s. It argues that leaders have a duty to focus primarily on meeting their team's needs rather than their own for the larger good of the organization. A good leader inspires and guides.

"But what the workforce finds inspiring today has undergone a change."

Today, playing the authority card of a 'boss' instantly invites disrespect and a mental note to look out for job openings at other organizations. Whereas a leader who is collaborative, communicative, empathetic, and trusting is deeply admired and followed. Until a few years ago in the near past, it sufficed to hold sufficient experience in a domain and thorough familiarity with company ethos to be leader material. Today, these qualities most likely weigh you down. People in leadership positions need to be specially trained in leadership and becoming well-versed in the outsider's perspective for the necessary rethink in workflows and SOP (standard operating procedures) strategies within the organization.

Gen Z and Gen Z-minded folks are picky when it comes to employers and what they receive from their jobs despite the rising news of layoffs and uncertainties. We need to reconsider the role of leaders in employee retention, but more importantly, company profitability.

> *"The core reason for investing in leadership training for any organization is not just to earn employee admiration. It is to help our business keep growing in the coming times."*

The rate at which we replace all traces of bossy leadership with servant styles of leadership across the organization will determine the quality of people we will be able to hire in the years to come and, consequently, the quality of our output and business growth.

If we see that we are fast headed to a world dominated by a Gen Z workforce, Gen Z clients, and Gen Z customers, we will not waste another minute to run a serious evaluation of our human resources, not just in terms of client satisfaction and domain experience but mostly in terms of managerial and leadership style.

No 'Boss'

CHAPTER IV

Every Person A Brand

Like a pinch of salt brings out the sweetness of sugar, a pinch of nostalgia makes us appreciate all that has changed that much more. Just 15–20 years ago, it was complicated for me to explain the exact nature of my job to people outside of the industry. A brand strategy planner. The engineers, doctors, scientists, and armed forces personnel in my extended family and friends' circle barely understood what a brand was and why it needed dedicated strategists to build.

Forget them; even key leaders within the ad agencies I worked at in the 2000s did not see the need to put in this much thought and scrutiny behind advertising campaigns. Strategy planning, which had emerged as a separate discipline, was in general met with hostility. Strategy planners were an inconvenient change in the system because they made creativity accountable. Utterly unnecessary. This is in line with the overarching theme of this book. It was a 'resistance to change.' Strategists had come out of nowhere and shifted the attention from industry opinion to the opinion of the population—those annoying nitwits for whom the creative communication was intended. In time, there has been a slow but steady acceptance of the need for the discipline of strategy to build great brands from all quarters of the ad agency. But something more interesting has happened in recent years.

In the afterglow of the digital revolution facilitating every individual with their own platform to showcase every day of their lives to the whole world, a new phenomenon has emerged: brand building for the self.

Each and every one of us is now a brand. And we can build it on the same principles on which conventional brands are built: with well-defined core ethos, capabilities, offering to the world, and differentiators. We each need to discover and articulate the essence of who we are, just like any good brand does, with consistency. Because whether or not we think of it strategically, a reputation is being built. An image is being constructed in the eyes of the beholder and potential buyer, employer, or partner. In this digital age, each of us is being beheld all the time. Those of us who prefer to keep off the grid also need to find avenues to build their personal brand in order to have choices and an advantage in this new world.

> "*The only difference between building a personal brand and a product brand is the idea of a 'competition' analysis. Personal brands don't have competition; they only have opportunities for collaboration.*"

We often hear people in the traditional workforce claim that they used to be good singers, good cooks, actors, sketch artists, or classical dancers until their mainstay careers took over. Today, we don't need to push a bunch of our skills into the past tense to be able to hold a job or run a business. A differentiated personal brand allows us to build on all our capabilities.

Personal branding is helping people be honest about who we are, who we want to be, and how we want to serve the world to earn a living. It enables us to find like-minded people to work with. People are learning how to build their personal brand to suit their own immediate and long-term pursuits and to gain from the abundance of opportunity and possibility the internet has opened up.

And just like that, brand building has gone from being a specialized skill deserving a separate department of experts for it, to being a foundational skill every professional needs to hone, no matter what their domain or work experience is. Personal brand building, like driving or cooking, is quickly turning into a basic life skill for anyone looking to navigate through life better.

*In this reality, it becomes imperative for product brand builders to acknowledge that the audience now knows the tricks of the brand-building trade. Gimmicks, messaging that has passed its expiry date, misleading labels, and vulnerability-exploiting advertising will be called out. We need to see that our audience **sees** us.*

Every Person A Brand

CHAPTER V

Post-Purchase Justification To Post-Purchase Pride

The year was 2010. I was employed at Publicis India in their Mumbai office. The then planning lead, Subramanayeswar S or Subbu, as he is popularly known and easier to pronounce, had implemented a simple initiative in the office. He had 1 office employee, irrespective of level or department, volunteer every Friday to make a showcase to the office on a subject that they personally loved. This was in acknowledgement of the fact that as creative professionals, it is useful to expand our horizons to subjects outside of our own interests. Each of us learned about passions other than our own. 14 years later, I still find the things that I learned in those sessions enriching my ideas. This is the power of good leadership. But, I already covered that in the chapter titled, 'no boss'.

Bear with me as I seemingly digress again, to tell you about the youngest person in that office, Pia Amonkar. She introduced us millennials to the world of Anime. I found it difficult to digest how someone could consider a cartoon with such seriousness. I know better now than to refer to anime as a cartoon. I have a better perspective today. Something very important for strategists.

Pia was also the first person I had met in an ad agency who was unlike anyone you'd find in those days in advertising circles. Ad folks back then, came in a set format – with our wit-offs (a term I coined to describe the exchanges where we try to outwit each other while also displaying how well-read we are or how well we know 70s rock) and our partying more than our salaries allowed, and flashing brands we couldn't afford yet. You know, just to maintain the enigma around ad industry folks. Are they happy or not? Are they smarter than us or not? Are they rich or not? Are they glamorous or not? In this world, I meet Pia, the youngest fresher in our office with no hesitation to buy a phone from a brand called Micromax.

Micromax, for non-Indian readers, is an Indian manufacturer of consumer electronics and home appliances, headquartered in Gurugram, advertised as being low-cost. For context, this was 2010. A time when, at least among us ad folks, there was great embarrassment attached to being seen in denim jeans that were not Lee, Levi's, or Pepe. Even if it meant that we owned just one pair of jeans for years. Perfumes had to be of luxe brands like CK or Davidoff, at least. You get the drift. A next-gen person in the same milieu with no qualms about using a Micromax phone was met with some frowns. Some behind her back. But she didn't care one bit. According to her, it was a great phone and was cheap. She saw no reason to spend lots just for show-off value. Most of us in the office playfully made fun of her, but she didn't seem to be bothered at all. As a matter of fact, she was proud of her choice. Still, as a 28-year-old in 2010, I remember thinking that I would never be seen with a brand that advertises its inexpensive-ness. Buying a low-cost brand had to be done in secret. At all costs.

How times have changed and suddenly at that. In 2015, I bought my first Xiaomi phone, also known for being low-cost and having no flash value as such. It served my needs more than satisfactorily. When people with their expensive phones saw me be happy with my purchase, some would remark that I was smart and that they should have also just bought a Xiaomi and used the saved money for something else. Most users of high-end devices end up using only the basic features. They buy them for the flash value and the now fading notion that if it's expensive, it must be better. Those who buy expensive brands without much research have to look for post-purchase justification. Those who buy low-costing, locally manufactured products for quality that exceeds expectations bask in post-purchase pride. Because their purchase decision is a result of their own research.

> "*Flash-value is being replaced by recommendation-value.*"

I later went on to buy a Micromax TV. My neighbor with an identical looking TV that he bought for 10 times the price insisted that this was a poor choice. The pun was perhaps intended. But it wasn't a bad choice. The TV served me well for 3 years since, until I sold it when I had to move cities. 2 years ago, in 2022, when I had to buy new sports shoes, I made the bold step to try out an inexpensive brand. A once upon a time sacrilege as big as being seen in local brands of denim jeans. (Which also I am now. Have been for close to a decade.) I am delighted with getting the same quality Nike had given me for years, for 10% of the price. I tried out a robotic vacuum cleaner from Kerala-born Ibell 4 years ago. Zero complaints. Perhaps, I am just a Gen Z-minded old person. But I am not alone.

This trend reflects in the silent rise of Indie brands across categories from beauty, F&B, fashion to perfumes. I was working on a leading HUL hair care brand 4 years ago. They mandated us to keep a hawk's eye on Wow Skin Science and report back on how they had managed to wow their customers from under their nose.

With the proliferation of social media, the facility to search and access information, and the provision to co-write the life story of brands, customers themselves have become the chief influencers of culture and choice. The tables have turned. This is a generation that is not above making frugality cool. Recycling is up-cycling. Vogue India described it as, 'they want canteen but make it luxe'. In this new, possibly confusing world order, vanity stems from substance, not image-building advertising alone.

There is no pride in buying a very expensive brand that provides exactly the same quality as a brand that is offering it for 1/10th the price. An iPhone still has flash value, mainly because it offers superior quality in photography and filming in a phone. But, consider Titan Eye Plus Vs Lenskart in India. Titan Eye Plus has swanky showrooms that resemble jewelry outlets and are priced accordingly. They offer 'vanity-value' to their customers. On the other hand, Lenskart works on providing 'pride-value'. It feeds the sense of feeling smarter for availing a variety of compliment-drawing looks with decent quality along with their staple buy-one-get-one offer. The upcoming generation of customers are drawn to choices that make them proud of their smart research behind their purchase decisions.

Shopping = Researching Online

CHAPTER VI

Loyalty to Brand Open-Relationships

American blues musician, who goes by the stage name Little Axe, is known to have said, "If you want loyalty, get a dog," poignantly illustrating the futility of seeking loyalty in a disloyal world. Regardless, a lot of us are obsessed with loyalty, not just in human relationships but also in marketing strategies. The only trouble is that, with everything other than dogs, setting out to measure its loyalty is asking to be disappointed. This applies to the idea of 'brand loyalty' too.

Prem Narayan, national planning head, Ogilvy India, had suggested the book, "How Not to Plan" to his team, of which I was fortunate to be a part. First published in 2018, its authors, Les Binet and Sarah Carter, point out that failure to improve brand loyalty is not just an advertising problem. It's been estimated that 2/3 of all CRM (customer relationship management) programs fail too. One wonders why.

Chasing the objective of building brand loyalty may have been relevant in simpler times when there were 2 choices the audience had in any given domain. Today, analysis paralysis and FOMO (fear of missing out) caused by an overload of choices has become the reality. Our audience wants to try it all out. It is about time we stopped fumbling with our eyes closed for brand loyalty.

Today, more than ever before, most of a brand's users are experimenting with other brands simultaneously. This is mirrored in human relationships as well, with concepts of 'situationships,' 'polyamory,' and 'open relationships' picking up. The notion of loyalty seems to have undergone a corresponding change.

If I understand right, loyalty today may be understood as a give and take of honesty. It does add up. Loyalty or honesty are not supposed to be a Herculean task. The only honesty that matters is the kind that comes easy. Honesty stems from the sense that we will understand and work around confusions, even if it means the need to give the other some space of their own.

No matter the category, there are many brands people want to try, for the novelty, promise, backstory, sustainability practices, and not to forget, lower prices for a premium offering. This is irrespective of whether or not they are satisfied with the experience of their existing choices.

> "*The biggest favor we can do ourselves, in a 'brand open relationship' world, would be to be one of the top favorites. For this, as Gen Z would put it, vibes need to match.*"

It's a 'confused with choices' world. Vibes become our final resort to help us decide. Some brands feel good. We like them. We hear about them being talked about for delivering reliable products and services. The news we hear about them makes us respect them. On the contrary, word about being a toxic employer, and/or a poor work ethic, and/or leaving an adverse effect on the environment, and/or tone-deaf brand narratives make for a negative vibe. A good product with great advertising alone no longer helps brands make the cut for being a chosen brand. A great product with good advertising always will. But, when things get confusing, the brand with the better vibe gets picked.

The natural response of brands gunning for brand loyalty tends to be to scramble for creative ways of exploiting FOMO anxiety. What we need to see is that our customers are seeking avenues to feel less anxious, not more.

> *"As brands, we need to proactively showcase good intentions. We need to be stress-relieving, not stress-exploiting."*

What if we start accepting that customers want to try out other brands and demonstrate that we are ok with it? Then, we aim for building the vibe of being the brand that consistently is helpful, delightful, comforting, enriching, inspiring, and leaves people feeling better every time they engage with us—being the brand that is unconditionally bought and advocated, despite any number of flings.

> *A realistic and fairly measurable goal would be to 'build stronger brand vibes with the audience' instead of 'build brand loyalty.' This will make us use our creative juices to identify how we can cultivate our words and actions as a company via our brand advertising and content to heighten the chances of our TG (target group) to want to spend time with us, feel comfortable with us, engage more with us, and thereby buy us more than they do other brands.*

Loyalty Seekers

CHAPTER VII

Gen Z and Millennials at Loggerheads

Some research reports club findings about Gen Z with those about millennials. As a millennial myself, this feels a bit off-key. You know, the 10 odd years that separate the two cohorts? Those 10 years were not like any other ordinary set of 10 years. That was the decade, we went from just WWW (world wide web) to WWW with search engines. From chat windows to social networks. From standing in queues to online booking. From those preciously rare meet-cutes IRL (in real life) to on-demand swipe rights. Millennials felt this shift. We felt it. Many are still reeling from the impact. Gen Z was born into the already shifted world. This makes us far more 'different' than research reports which club us together suggest. No wonder that Gen Z is largely a mystery, even for most millennials who are just about 10 years older on average.

"This closeness in age but vast gap in life experience makes for a tumultuous dynamic between Gen Z and millennials."

The following 5 areas where the clash is apparent can help researchers and communication strategists stay in the picture:

Career: I can speak for most millennials living in India, when I say that while we did have greater opportunities to pursue beyond the conventional options, we still always had to first apply for engineering, medicine, chartered accountancy or at least, for a degree in computer applications, before setting out to explore options that seemed to be opening up for us. If we passed the entrance test, we typically spent 3-5 years obtaining the degree first, however unrelated it was to what we really wanted to pursue. Just 10 years down, parents of Gen Z kids became okay with their kids exploring careers of their choice from the start even if it was something new-fangled like a full-time indie musician or travel vlogger. This age advantage makes them completely different from millennials who mostly bloomed later in life, that is if we ever did.

Marriage: By the early 2000s, parents of teens had ceased to be the enemy in mainstream cinema, which focused on friendships and family bonds with a love story woven in. This coincided with the times when research revealed a surge in young urban Indians choosing love-arranged or outright arranged marriage because of the trust they have in their parents and family. A stark difference from the attitudes of just 5 years prior. Going by popular cinema of the mid to late 90s, love marriages were an act of rebellion and revolution against a 'zamana' (loosely translated, society) touted as being enemies of love. Most millennials still find the idea of adults being close friends with their parents hard to swallow. Whereas most Gen Zers are actual pals with their parents. Many parents somehow grew understanding and supportive with their second-born as opposed to the same people with their older millennial kids.

Attitude toward being judged: Gen Z is unfazed by allegations of being privileged and lazy. The generation most irked by this attitudinal empowerment of Gen Z are millennials, who have just got where they have after at least a decade of putting office, family expectations, and a need for societal validation before self.

Mental health: Millennials need greater coaxing to be convinced that there indeed is no taboo in acknowledging our vulnerabilities and seeking help for it. We used to be wary of people with known mental disorders. Gen Zers, on the other hand, are wary of people who have never been to therapy. They are the ones who tend to lack insight and be callously harsh and insensitive and laugh if you pointed it out.

Life philosophy: Gen Z only knows of a world that keeps giving them more chances. Something we millennials did not have in our formative years. The cost of error in present times is close to nil. Gen Z is unafraid to give anything a go, even if ill-prepared. Millennials, on the other hand, have to first overcome the fear of failing and 'looking' stupid.

Targeting the age group of 20-30 years is no longer just about learning their lingo and gestures. Till 10 years ago, that would have worked because the rest fell in place as their realities were not hugely different from previous generations who had lived through the same age. What we need to see is that Gen Z reality is nothing like that of anybody who lived their age in an earlier time.

Millennials Vs Gen Z

32

CHAPTER VIII

'Smart' Fatigue

Have you ever lamented about having to deal with idiots all the time? Well, you are not alone. We have all been obsessed with smartness probably since the beginning of human existence. If lore is to be believed, Albert Einstein's wish to be cremated without ceremony was fulfilled but not before his brain was stolen to be researched. Doctors wanted to unravel the mysteries of the genius brain. This sums up our fascination with intelligence. We sliced it, quantified it, qualified it, carefully deconstructed it, and now we have... wait for it... re-constructed it! We have now reached the era where anything can be programmed to have an IQ (intelligence quotient). From beauty products to consumer durables to automobiles to wearables, they are all urging us to experience their 'smartness' in some capacity or other.

> *"We are in awe of intelligence, even if it is artificial. Only trouble is, gee whiz, we are now overwhelmed by it and wishing it went away."*

Something we never imagined could be possible. The 1994 film 'Dumb and Dumber' made us laugh at the stupidity fest, but now people are beginning to crave some dumb. Nostalgically yearning to go back to the way things once were. 10 years ago.

It takes a lot of work to detox from the dopamine rush our smartphones have got us addicted to. This has caused the Kafkaesque irony of people seeking ways to escape 'smartness'. The once considered finished brick-phone market is witnessing a revival. Fondly termed as dumb phones, they are being loved for their simplicity and physical sturdiness. There seems to be a certain reliability in dumb phones that smartphones had us compromise on.

It is not just with telecommunications. For decades, vinyl had been pushed away to attics or second-hand shops by devices so smart that all you need to do is give a 'voice command' to listen to what you want. No need to place a spindle in the right position or press a 'play' button. Most of the time, the device hears you right. It definitely does in a few attempts. Mostly. And yet, today we are witnessing a revival of vinyls. Samanvii Digimedia Art and Solutions Pvt Ltd just opened India's first vinyl record manufacturing plant in over four decades, suggesting that analogue is desired again.

Another area where smart technology is being dropped is dating. Smart dating apps revolutionized the landscape of romance but also complicated it beyond belief. Leaving us to grapple with concepts of 'situationships' and 'non-exclusivity', among others. Not to mention falling prey to scams and disappointments which could easily have been avoided but for smart dating apps. Little surprise that they have been losing their appeal in recent years. A UK-based startup called Pear has addressed these concerns by helping single people meet each other offline. All they need to do is wear an aqua-colored ring, made by Pear, to show their openness to being wooed. US-born Thursday, an IRL (in real life) dating brand, says on their website, *"f*ck dating apps. I am better in-person."* They organize in-person events for singles every Thursday. The idea is so simple, it's almost dumb. At the time of writing this piece, they have expanded their service to 250 cities.

Having said that, AI is not going anywhere and already is an integral part of our life. SEO (search engine optimization) is making way for AEO (answer engine optimization), i.e., optimization of what we ask ChatGPT. AI virtual influencers are already so real, they are ready to replace models in ads films. We are heading for a smart-overloaded world and in such a world, people will tend to love good old dumbness like never before.

Victims of smart-fatigue, people are craving simpler technologies. In the right measure, dumb in products, brands, and communications may indeed be smart.

Smart Fatigue

CHAPTER IX

Jokes Are Not A Joking Matter

When the world operated largely in binary, it was a harsher world, but things were simpler. We win some, we lose some, as they say. People of Gen Z mindsets are more than happy to embrace this complexity in exchange for the opportunity to explore and be accepted for who they are. This includes their mental and physical vulnerabilities, sexual ambiguities, and overall societal wins and losses. People with an older bend of mind tend to have one other lament from this mindset change other than the loss of simplicity, and that is—the loss of freedom to joke unthinkingly. Really tragic.

This new way of thinking has made jokes themed around body weight, gender, skin colour, caste, race, and extreme poverty, etc., inappropriate. This is depriving a lot of people of their entire public personality and charm. It is stripping them of the only comic material that worked well for them for decades. Don't be sad. It doesn't look like the celebrations on the other side of the fence are bereft of internal conflict.

While individuality is being facilitated by the new world order of things, we are still as stuck as ever in the spider web of needing to belong. In other words, be followed, engaged with, and be widely shared. Social media app algorithms are perhaps pushing people into a straight line as they wander off in various directions in their respective existential pursuits. We have the resources to easily find validation for our fingerprint identity, but at the same time, we are also forced to follow set regimes to be able to access that validation. A validation, the absence of which makes us susceptible to falling down a lonely rabbit hole. That can't be fun. Unless it leads to mad and unexpected adventures, which is known to happen too.

> "*Social media apps are at the same time the generator of this storm and also the guardrails for it. The jokes, good and objectionable, are cracked and ripped apart on the same platforms.*"

It is debatable whether social media catalyzed this change in our attitude to jokes or not, but there are no two opinions on the matter that social media connections are fuelled by humour. Safer to go with humour that is self-deprecating or punches-up, not down. We need to see the dynamics of what makes a joke problematic to a more globally aware, open, and mindful generation.

The challenge is to make our messaging across platforms 'on brand' while being 'on platform' to truly become a brand 'on fleek'. Being 'on platform' may require an understanding of how humour works on social media. Consumer brands will need to re-work their brand playbook and make it a truly playful one.

Jokes Are Not A Joking Matter

CHAPTER X

The Revolution In Consumerism

The term 'consumerism' has multiple and conflicting definitions. This article uses the one that refers to a culture of excessive buying beyond what is needed, encapsulated in a quote credited to American actor Edward Norton: "*We buy things we don't need, with money we don't have, to impress people we don't like.*" This culture of blind buying is fueled by the advertising and marketing efforts of companies that directly benefit from the insecurities of consumers, leading them to spend more. However, today, something interesting is happening.

A vault has been yanked open for consumers to use at their own discretion. Constant and easy access to seemingly basic knowledge that was previously kept away from end-consumers is now easily and readily available. What's more, the end consumer, who traditionally only was at the receiving end, now has the facility of broadcasting what they now think and know, quicker than conventional broadcasters of information did. The consumer is no longer a sitting recipient of the shiniest, loudest, most emotional, most entertaining communication by advertisers. They have the tools to do their own study and come to their own conclusions – whether they are right or wrong – they need not align to the narrative set by mighty companies.

It is like the consumer is being snapped out of decades of hypnotism. Moreover, with the advocacy of self-love and self-acceptance on the rise, people don't rely on brands to feel validated or worthy anymore. A new kind of consumerism is unfolding, championed by the conscious consumer. They have no business interest. They are simply concerned about how the things they consume have been affecting them as a people, their children, and the environment. With consumers reading ingredient lists and with an emerging willingness to buy the new, less expensive brand as long as it offers comparable quality and premium imagery, or alternately, the willingness to buy the more expensive brand for a promise of clean quality, we are witnessing a revolution in consumerism. There is also a rising set of consumers who are increasingly willing to take on varying degrees of inconvenience to decrease the negative impacts of their decisions on the environment or their own health. In the least, people are becoming vigilant of the impact of their decisions.

"Retail therapy was good, but now it has led to clutter."

A clutter of bags, shoes, books, clothes, kitchenware, home linen, junk jewelry, makeup, skin care, stationery. The joy of all the things mentioned in that last sentence is all diminished by the one word – clutter. An unwanted byproduct of consumerism. Even for us marketers, the biggest challenge we have to deal with is market-clutter. No wonder then that today, psychologists are exploring the therapeutic benefits of the opposite of retail therapy – of letting go of excess – and living a minimalist lifestyle. People who find themselves stuck with overwhelming schedules, bursting closets, or a restless mind are drawn to the idea of trying to live with less — fewer social commitments, fewer possessions, and fewer distractions.

Some people see that change is opportunity. Skincare brand, Minimalist, built an INR 100 crore business within 8 months of inception in 2020. Clearly, they got more than just their naming right. The brand offers a curated range of clean & effective products designed to simplify beauty regimens. The operative word here being 'clean.' Most newly formed companies offer 'clean' – be it food, personal care, or beverages. Speaking of which, while India is poised for a revolution in cola pricing with the re-introduction of Campa Cola by Reliance Industries, we are also experiencing an unmistakable movement against sugary drinks making its way beyond the urban elite and major metros. That doesn't mean this is the end of junk F&B (food and beverage). It just means that we need to be honest in our labeling and advertising. Acknowledge and address the need we are catering to, instead of cueing to be harmless for health when consumed in copious amounts. The new consumer can see through that masquerade.

This has led to the growth of a phenomenon called de-influencing. De-influencers are social media users who discourage consumers from buying products that are alleged to be severely bad for the body, ineffective, not worth the money, or are secretly damaging the environment. The tug of war between companies placing their bets on blind consumerism and the emerging trend of consumers hellbent on opening their eyes promises interesting challenges and opportunities for businesses in the times to come.

Not all products we sell are healthy, women empowering, or planet preserving. That's ok. The idea is to sell what we sell without cueing lies. 31-year-old de-influencer Revant Himatsingka, who goes by the social media handle @foodpharmer, for example, is not against processed food but exposes processed food masquerading as healthy. We don't need to find loopholes to lie. Instead, we could deploy on-brand content strategy to provide value via relevant fan engagement and showcase genuine intent to help/inspire/ motivate/make life convenient, to name a few.

The Revolution In Consumerism

BUSINESSES ARE
CHANGING

CHAPTER XI

New-age Founders – A Product Of The Consumer Revolution

Do you remember the famous 'sell me this pen' scene from the 2013 film, The Wolf of Wall Street? Shockingly, the protagonist is compared to a wolf. Ok, that's not what's shocking. What is shocking today, is that it was universally accepted that salespersons are the ones who have the sharper acumen or the hunting instinct of a wolf which they use to prey on the lamb-like public to get richer. It is shocking that this was the status quo.

If you are a brand custodian or a marketer in any capacity, chances are that you are educated in several famous case studies of brands that carved a big share of the market for themselves against all odds. The main odd being that the target audience didn't see value in the offering, right away. Stories of how brands made product set-backs seem like an advantage or turned largely ordinary features into compelling wants have impressed us with their genius. It was genius. In a different time.

Marketers have been expert line blurrers. The lines between wants and needs. Turning whatever they are selling into needs. However, this did not make actual consumer needs disappear. Those remained and grew bigger to the point of a whole generation of independent entrepreneurs taking matters into their own hands, the minute they could.

This new wave of enterprises have been mushrooming and thriving in the evergreen forests of giant, legacy household brand names. These mushrooms have simply responded to the audience and cared to R&D (research and development) ways to cater to those needs. Needs such as cutting down on sugar without compromise on enjoyment, representing the majority Indian's complexion beyond the 'aspirational' very light skin, products for hair types other than smooth, 10 min home delivery of daily groceries, comparison of costs of any service be it travel, courier or life insurance. These are all businesses that are also built for profit.

> *"The difference is that new-age founders see buyers as allies as opposed to sitting ducks for hunting."*

This enterprise-renaissance is the result of the enablement of the end consumer with choices, information and ease of verification. All an individual needs to start their own business today, is a computer with internet connection and a product to sell. Along with the usual qualties of dedication, discipline, perseverance and hard-work.

Suddenly, the convenient-for-marketters view of the general public as vulnerable, emotional fools is smashed. The desire of the larger public is not the same as that of the handful of business tycoons. The latter is fundamentally motivated by profiteering at any cost. The former majority simply wants to live good and let live good. The latter is never truly able to understand the simple motivations of the former because of how different they are in their very nature. However, now that ratio between the tycoons and the people is shifting. The new generation of businesses are being built for good. They make profits and get rich too but by products that fulfill actual needs, which there is no shortage of.

I mentioned Wow Skin Science earlier in this book. Born in 2013, they are currently a bestselling brand on Amazon India and the USA. The brand's success is attributed to delivering beyond what trusted legacy brands regurgitated in India in the same formats of product and advertising for decades. WOW like may other indie brands offered a refreshing breath of novelty (which the masses were clearly ready for contrarary to the assesssment of established brands) and also leveraged new age ways of connecting with people across all tiered cities. Other brands that have captured audience advocacy with research founded, low-gimmick, innovation led brands include Dr. Sheth, Minimalist and Ordinary. Many are strategically packaged as premium but fairly accessible to a wide cross section of socio economic backgrounds.

> *"New-age founders are responding to the consumer shift from buying mainly into aspiration to buying mainly into the product itself."*

On the other hand, ed tech company Byju's formed in 2011 that operated like traditional profit hounds lost favor within a decade of existance.

Every new age brand that survived in the last 2 decades be it Oyo Rooms, The Whole Truth, The Wellness Co and several others don't appear like wolves. They are case studies in profit making entities in the new world order by building themselves a reputation doing good. Employee wellbeing is a matter of continued scrutiny and we are witnessing a rise in conversations in that area as well.

> *Being new-age ready requires a concerted effort to inculcate a style of functioning that is Gen Z-mindset dominant at both the business end as well as at the*

marketting and brand building end. This means pushing non-gen Z minded people to open their minds to themselves reap the benefits of the same as well.

Catering To Needs > Creating Needs

CHAPTER XII

The Turned Tables of Employer-Employee Dynamic

The traditional baits have gone rotten. For the first time, even the biggest, most sought-after employers are scratching their heads over how to attract and retain the worthy younger workforce. Without killing them. Literally. There is only one carrot that seems to matter today – a balanced work culture. Not just on the website but actually lived.

Tough ask from companies that have always been acclimated to a system where the employer has an upper hand over employees regardless of the technicality that they are bound by a fair contract where one party contributes to the profits of the other and the other offers a disproportionately less monetary compensation. The level of concern employers face over developing a reputation of an abnormal attrition rate is nothing compared to the level of fear employees feel of being fired or forming a reputation of jumping too many jobs.

"Who does this lopsided system really serve? A new generation of workforce is asking."

The rants often heard during lunch breaks at office building cafeterias can be summarized as this: the aim of any business is to make profits and grow, but does this warrant dealing with an environment of narcissistic managers who feel almost duty-bound to be careless about employee health or to intentionally push organizational stress levels to a steady boiling point? This is what Gen Z and people with a Gen Z mindset see. Once we *see* it this way, it is hard to unsee.

Looking back, in my career spanning 20 years across at least 5 leading and two mid-sized companies, I have directly and indirectly witnessed managers who seem to take it as a personal shortcoming to see anyone on their team delivering on expectation confidently while managing to balance personal pursuits with work. The goalpost is proactively adjusted to ensure sheer mental exhaustion. Encouragement and rewards, not monetary but by way of preferential treatment, is showered on people who minimize on a good night's rest and ignore personal health. This often means starting to smoke and abuse alcohol to cope or coming to work with neck collars despite the doctor's orders to be on bed rest or missing funerals and weddings of loved ones. Such behaviors were and perhaps still are proactively glorified.

That super-senior manager who is a permanent fixture in the office at any time of day, night, or holiday, scoffing at youngsters for aspiring towards work-life balance, is the one promoted to the highest position in the years to come. Intentionally or unintentionally sending out a clear message to anyone holding ambitions of getting promoted within a corporate organization. What we see is that it is not just commitment that is rewarded but a consistent sacrifice of our personal existence in its entirety that helps break ceilings. This suits a small percentage of the workforce well. The lucky few whose personal lives align perfectly with this sort of demand from employers. For the large majority, it certainly seems like they are in an eternal cycle to somehow complete 1-3 years in a given place of employment to then move to a new place hoping to find a more humane employer-ethic. The ones who stay on, see their chief accomplishment as being able to survive this system. Whether they choose to remain good souls or turn into antagonizer-in-chief is a different matter. The odd good manager/mentor is seen as an anomaly that the people working for feel eternally blessed for. As I have been a few times in my career. Far fewer than ideal.

The Gen Z minded see that unlike their immediately senior counterparts, they are born into a world with the actual provision to *not* have to sacrifice your existence to make a living, make millions, or to be in leadership roles.

> *"There is no escaping the fact that every individual today is empowered to put in all that hard work into their own enterprise of any size. Leaving only the terribly low self-esteemed and diffident workforce to stay on in toxic workplaces for long. Quality resources move on."*

There are countless stories of people of all age groups and from all socio-economic backgrounds who quit unpleasant corporate work environments to start earning similar or far greater amounts by setting up something for themselves, often with zero capital. The opportunities are endless.

This is shattering the archaic structure of employment slowly but surely. There continues to be a dark abyss between what companies claim about their employer-ethic and what really is lived out. Explaining the maddening attrition rate. Even while blaming it on the entitled, privileged mindset of the young workforce, companies are now scrambling to build an image of being empathetic employers. Companies have started to think about their reputation more than employees worry about theirs. The tables have turned.

As Gen Z slowly but surely forms the majority of the workforce, only those who insist on balancing personal time off and work time are being admired. Anyone who is sacrificing family time, health, and other hobbies entirely for the office in the name of a 'passion' for a corporate entity is slowly beginning to feel like a foolish rat. Companies will have to not just accommodate but proactively promote work-health balance to retain a sensible workforce.

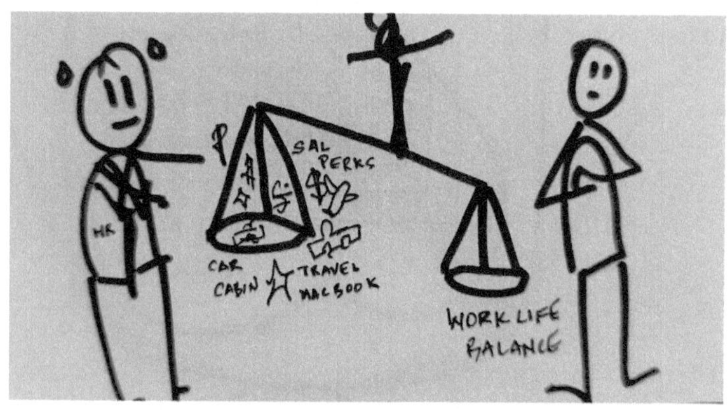

The Imbalance

CHAPTER XIII

The Smashing of 'Business As Usual'

Working from home was an outlandish notion just 5 years ago, in the beginning of 2020. The year Covid-19 started to raise its ugly head, a few companies were quick to start working out logistics to facilitate WFH (work from home). Others took a little longer to incorporate them. And then there were companies that simply waited for the crisis to pass to return to 'business as usual'. This was till the number of deaths caused by the pandemic hit the roof, a long year down the line. In the same vein, as soon as the lockdown ended, some companies eagerly returned to business as usual with zero appreciation for the impact the lockdown had on people and zero tolerance to hybrid work models. Never mind productivity, efficiency, costs, safety, and employee choice.

As per an article published in The Economic Times in 2021, a survey by a prominent research institute revealed that in India, close to 86 percent of the surveyed companies reported increased productivity levels since the shift to hybrid working. Over 90 percent of Indian employers agreed that employees should be given the right to request flexible working from day one. A 2021 Gartner Survey revealed that 50% of Indian hybrid workers consider themselves more productive when working remotely.

In response, several companies completely shifted to working from home. Many others embraced the hybrid model and continue to smooth out glitches every day. And then there are those that focus all their energies into justifying the need to return to 'business as usual' - just the way it was before all this pandemic nonsense. This entailed what we covered in the previous chapter: sacrificing personal existence in its entirety to be present physically for meetings and brainstorms, neck-collars and viral illnesses notwithstanding. Taking 20 cigarette breaks throughout the day and ending a laboriously unproductive day with a drink at the nearby watering hole.

> *"'Business as usual' shifts the focus from quality of output back to reckless effort. Ah! the golden days."*

Change, even when we stand to gain from it, is not easy to work around. There have been more instances of digital transformation failure. Often, because it is insincerely handled as a side operation to flank the main 'business as usual' operations. The new world order warrants the reinvention of a company's culture, processes, and technology. It can be a daunting process, but organizational intent and attitude make all the difference.

Today brands and businesses are being researched by people. Arguably more thoroughly than people have ever been researched by businesses. This has disrupted the usual notion of what determines success for a business. The skill of selling anything using clever manipulation is no longer what assures business success. Why? Because the digital era has unraveled a world where it is possible to find and sell useful products to exactly those who need it, on demand from and to anywhere. This is what has led to unprecedented growth for businesses that transformed successfully or for businesses that were born in this era.

> *"And so business success metrics are expanding beyond just sales reports. Today, the reputation of*

a company for its relevance in the new-age - that is being empathatic to employees and buyers, being considerate about sustainability, becoming conversant with what 'toxicity a the work place' means and understanding brand strategy in the new-age media landscape - forms a big chunk of what determines the success of a company."

When even commerce has moved nearly completely online or gone phy-gital, what is continuing to make many companies feel crippled without showing up daily in the office? What does this handicap say about the management, when it is cost and time-efficient for both the employer and employees to adopt a working hybrid model? Not to mention the companies that claim to be hybrid only on paper, strictly not in reality. Is it solely the mindsets of inert leadership that are slowing down this incredible transformation that could actually allow people to have a life while also contributing to the profits of a corporate entity?

We can slow it down, but we cannot stop it. The future of quality work is hybrid and output-focused.

The Mindlessness Of Reckless Effort

CHAPTER XIV

Sustainability Becomes Profitable

In 2010, the global shampoo brand I worked on highlighted the fact that they used less plastic in their bottles in other markets but didn't believe it mattered to their TG (Target Group) audience in India. I was clearly not their primary TG, and this was very disappointing. Not that I was not their TG, but that the larger shampoo-using segment in the country did not care about the environment as much as they did about their hair.

Cut to 2024, the awareness and consciousness about the impact of our day-to-day actions and choices are slowly but surely seeping into larger India. In 2021, Nivea launched their Naturally Good range in India, with Taapsee Pannu as their ambassador. The advertisement says, '*good for nature, good for you,*' giving equal weightage to the fact that they used 50% less plastic in their packaging and the product quality. Needless to say, I was delighted with the development, as it meant the larger India was aligning with my way of thought. I don't have data on how this campaign impacted the fortunes of Nivea, but it definitely means that sustainability has started to matter in some way or the other.

The role of sustainability in the business growth strategy becomes more pronounced in an ecosystem where brands need to front-load with intent, authenticity, and purpose to make themselves vibe better with an evolving audience. One of the ways to care for our audience is to safeguard and help heal their planet, which incidentally is all of our planet. For some reason, when it was declared that the purpose of business is to make profit, no one showed the vision to see that everyone faces losses if the planet and its resources are depleted at a rate faster than it can repair.

Today, 'sustainability' has permeated as a concept not just in business but also in the business of advertising and marketing for business. Billboards and digital signages, for example, are moving towards being solar-powered, using recycled material or plant-based structures to integrate into the natural ecosystem, etc. It will be a matter of time when we see further innovations such as what McDonald's in Sweden did in 2019, when they replaced their traditional backlit billboards with habitats for bees. This creative, multi-use billboard exemplified how advertising can be integrated into the environment. In the Philippines, Coca-Cola created billboards made from recycled PET bottles. These conversation-stirring displays not only promoted recycling but also demonstrated a commitment to reducing plastic waste. Much-needed, as the awareness about Coca-Cola being the world's largest contributor to branded plastic waste will only spread more in the years to come.

It is understandable that brands with some pre-existing bad karma tend to act faster than the rest. But, no matter what the business, incorporating sustainable practices and initiatives into the brand story does not just offset our actions but has actually become profitable.

What drives the consumer into leaning towards sustainable brand choices? On some level, it is guilt mixed with intent. People are unable to adopt sustainable practices in day-to-day life owing to the higher cost and inconvenience it could incur. This is most apparent from the fact that fruit and vegetable vendors stock plastic bags, no matter the bans and restrictions enforced, because not providing plastic bags has a direct impact on their daily sales. Buyers demand plastic bags, sometimes more than one per customer. This seems to contradict everything in this chapter, but bear with me.

"People do seek convenient ways to be sustainable. That is where brands can and need to help."

In a choice-overloaded marketplace causing constant dilemmas, a simple factor like being environmentally friendly could tip the bets in favor of a brand.

Even though sustainability serves all of us, both at an individual level and at a business entity level, we sidelined it because it did not impact P&Ls. Now, this stands changed. As climate change anxiety rises, people seek convenient ways of doing their part. Brands that do it for them stand to gain favor. We need to assist buyers in supporting environmental initiatives, generating less waste, and with recycling ideas.

People are helping themselves to brands that help them help the planet.

Sustainability Becomes Profitable

CHAPTER XV

Turning Circular

It has been a while since businesses started adopting pro-environmental practices. Of course, motivations are often limited to the need for policy and regulation compliance or driven by the need to dilute the damage caused to corporate reputation, which in turn is caused by the damage they have caused to the environment. Take fashion, for instance. Fashion looks pretty, but fashion production alone makes up 10% of humanity's carbon emissions, dries up water sources, and pollutes rivers and streams. And so, fashion brands are recognizing their role in the pressing threat of limited resources. Today, a brand like Patagonia that first made its commitment to the environment in 1986 by adopting a circular model is no longer an outlier.

A circular business is one step ahead of adopting sustainable practices. It is a system where the entire cycle of the business, from the manufacture of an item to the end of its life, is equally important. The aim is to prevent waste by intentionally designing items to be reusable, repairable, biodegradable, and recyclable. The concept envisions industry as an almost endless circle in which materials are kept in use for as long as possible.

Patagonia's Worn Wear program, which started around a decade ago, offers to repair your Patagonia clothing, and if the clothing is beyond repair, it will recycle it for you. This has the additional benefit of staying meaningfully connected with their audiences for way longer than until when a purchase is made, encouraging further purchases. Win-win.

Innovation companies like Circ are collaborating with textile and fashion brands to help shape the future of fashion into a more circular one. To encourage and enable more of these, an innovation platform called Fashion for Good was set up 5 years ago to connect those working on sustainable innovation across the globe with brands, retailers, manufacturers, and founders. From polyester alternatives made from algae to blockchain technology making the supply chain more transparent – they have a network of innovators, each working on disruptive solutions to support circular fashion. Dutch company DyeCoo, which has partnerships with Nike and Ikea, has developed a process of dyeing cloth that uses no water at all, and no chemicals other than the dyes themselves. This is remarkable considering the textile industry is notorious for using vast quantities of water and chemicals and producing huge amounts of toxic waste.

Here in India, since 2019, entrepreneur and sustainability expert Saachi Bahl has hosted the 'Conscious Effort' conclave in New Delhi every year. The theme for 2023 was 'Innovation & Craftsmanship—Future of Sustainable Design.'

The focused attention the model got from the textile and fashion industry gave birth to the concept of 'circular fashion.' It is now officially cool to rethink existing systems for effective, profitable, win-win ways to embrace a circular economy.

"Environmental consciousness is the new health consciousness."

A presently small but growing number of people are being vigilant about where the things they buy come from, what they are made of, who made them, and being accountable for the overall lifecycle of their belongings.

A company's impact on the environment has gone from being about corporate social responsibility (CSR) to catering to the consumer's sense of social responsibility (CCSSR).

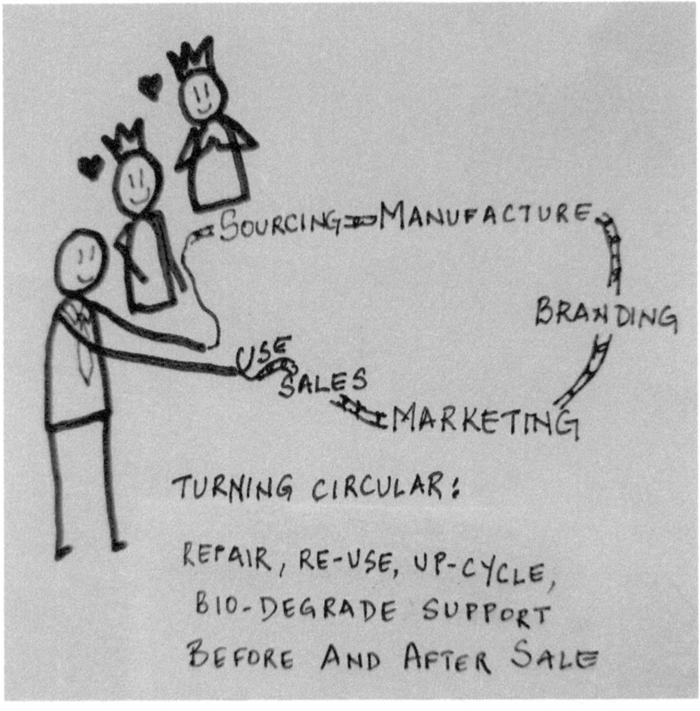

Catering To Consumer's Sense of Social Responsibility (CCSSR)

REALITIES ARE CHANGING

CHAPTER XVI

Everything, For Everyone

Back when I was introduced to the technicalities of operating an SLR camera, while studying for post-graduation from Symbiosis Institute of Media and Communications, Pune in 2002, photography was known as a millionaire's hobby because of the high costs involved in owning a camera, keeping a steady stream of film rolls, well, rolling in, and setting up a darkroom or paying a studio for film development. Even if one did invest in the hobby, it would be a long while, if at all, before their work was published somewhere or received public admiration. This was the reality till as recently as 2 decades ago, in 2003.

At that time, camera phones had already made an appearance in Korea, and the idea of people walking down streets clicking pictures on the go from their phones sounded straight out of a science fiction novel. In another 2 years, camera phones became fairly common in India as well. And in another 10 odd years, mobile phone cameras would start to pose an actual threat to the livelihoods of skilled SLR camera photographers.

In 2010, Instagram entered the scene. Turns out, when not expensive and tedious, *everyone* is a passionate photographer. As per Statista.com, as of January 2024, India alone had a total of 362 million Instagram users.

It is hard to think of a skill that has not had a similar journey in the last decade. The first blogging platform, Open Diary, started in 1998, making it possible for anyone to publish their own stories, ideas, and points of view and share them with the world, free from the gatekeepers who until then controlled what was worth publishing and what was not. Why, this book is being put together in the confidence that I can self-publish it. Social networking sites and dating apps give even the most introverted among us a fighting chance at the possibility of finding a companion. Easy video and image editing apps make it possible to develop brand communications from your home.

If there are no apps to do it for you, you can still learn any skill you put your heart to, from the convenience of your own home, often for free. YouTube makes learning how to do anything available to anyone in any part of the world. Be it laying the tiles in your bathroom, baking a cake in a mug, building your own business with an initial capital of INR 25,000, navigating the stock market, or crocheting.

> *"The democratisation of skill is changing how the world functions. We may vilify it or glorify it. Embrace it or fear it. But one thing we can't do is prevent absolutely anyone from benefiting from it."*

Generative AI is now making it all quicker, simpler, and cheaper. It throws open the gates to a new world order where the only skill that will truly matter is how well you adapt and use the tools that democratise skills to advance human output, ideally for collective progress.

Back when exclusivity was currency, the gatekeepers of success across industries slowed down the process of exploration, experimentation, and innovation.

> *"The advancement of technology has made way for a free, fearless exchange of ideas to be further amplified by like-minded people to collectively watch magic unfold."*

This has made way for a rejection of toxic insecurities, an appreciation for the uniquensss of every individual, a fearlessness to tap into every self-potential, and the building up of each other. This is changing the fundamentals of what defines our value as a human resource.

As marketers and advertisers, we have to keep in mind an audience who is empowered. Not that there are no pain-points left. The challenge today is to identify the new pain-points of our audience within this new reality. If the new reality is that they can do things themselves, the pain-point would perhaps be a sense of working in isolation. And so, brands could provide a means for community building with like-minded folks in the realm of the brand offering. This works equally for high-involvement customers like new moms and meme-snacking teens. To build strong brands, the annual campaign planning and the ongoing 'family building' initiatives need to be worked out together by the same team, or as one team. The silos have to disappear.

There is no brand building company today that has social media experts and traditional brand building experts in the same team to handle strategy across online and offline platforms. Legacy agencies struggle with executing this integration for a variety of reasons. Young content companies are performance metrics-oriented, which is a good thing. Just that it can be made better with an experienced brand strategist on board. There is an opportunity wide open for a start-up - a communications agency that offers simultaneous online and offline brand building expertise and execution with a team that sees things as they are without the baggage of the 'usual' approach.

The Customer Is King --> The Customer Is Empowered

CHAPTER XVII

Companies That Changed How The World Works

Uber, WhatsApp, Airbnb, Canva. There are many such game-changers born in the past decade. What is common to them? They were all born out of seemingly innocent questions. Why can't we hail a cab from our phone? Why can't phone calls and texts to family and friends be accessible for everyone from anywhere? Why can't we feel at home when we travel away from home? Why can't graphic designing be easier for everyone?

If you read their stories, you will find that, be it Uber founders, Travis Kalanick and Garrett Camp, WhatsApp founders Jan Koum and Brian Acton, Airbnb founders Brian Chesky, Joe Gebbia, Nathan Blecharczyk, or Canva founder Melanie Perkins, they were all driven by wanting to make useful products first before making money. And yet their companies witnessed explosive growth despite the unsurprising pushbacks and hurdles of being a trailblazer.

> *"They focused on improving the product and did not need advertising for their initial growth spurts."*

World-renowned marketing thought leader Sandeep Dayal, in his 2021 book, Branding Between the Ears, calls it the 'no-brainer' strategy – offering a product/service so useful and with such a compelling value proposition that they don't need additional persuasion. Many of these companies did, however, need reputation management to tackle controversies that are inevitable when challenging the status quo and when being the first mover with no prior lessons to lean on.

The founders were all in their 20s or 30s. They were all told repeatedly that their idea was downright stupid. And yet, the impact of Uber is so powerful that many find it financially savvy and more convenient to not own a car at all. The gesture of waving to hail a cab is probably unrecognizable to a whole generation and the ones to follow. Today, keeping in touch from different rooms in the same building or across continents costs the same. The very idea of being separated by distance is not even remotely close to what it used to be just 15 years ago, thanks to WhatsApp. With the anxiety of finding a decent, safe, budget-friendly place to stay being lifted, Airbnb overhauled the whole travel and tourism sector. Canva has effectively made designing our personal brand and, in many ways, even our destiny easy and accessible for anyone with access to the internet. Together, these companies, along with many others like them, have literally changed the world.

Three key new truths glaring at us:

Relevance trumps life experience: We have to resist our urge to 'correct' young people based on our experiences. Relevance comes naturally to the young workforce.

Intent impacts business above all else: Profits today come from a sincere desire to solve customer problems and make their lives and our collective futures better. Companies aiming for profits without having these in place are being called out.

The status quo is to question the status quo: Innocent questions are changing the world. All that's left to do is to cultivate the flexibility and openness within us to respect the questions and see things in a new way.

Each of these companies enabled a world that shares, connects, and collaborates more. They helped transform us from operating with a scarcity mindset to an abundance mindset. That changes everything.

New-Age Founders

CHAPTER XVIII

Seeing Is Disbelieving

Deepfakes – it is coincidental that this portmanteau of 'deep learning' and 'fake' could also connote fakeness to its very depths. The irony lies in the fact that, just about 10 years ago, a concept that stirred quite the storm among us was 'authenticity'. A concept championed by the growing number of people who became online stars with nothing but their own genuine selves. This shift created cracks in the concrete templates set by traditional gatekeepers of entertainment and mass communication, making them crumble.

It became clear that people are drawn to realness. A realness that acknowledges and embraces its own vulnerabilities and flaws. In response, every entity, whether brands, businesses, or celebrities, that sought to connect with people, presented their authentic selves, contributing to the deglorification of unrealistic standards. Things became more human. Then, suddenly, generative AI entered the scene.

Generative AI, with its growing popularity on social media and digital communication platforms, is making 'authenticity' seem outdated. Very last decade. In this case, things haven't even evolved along the same path as the last decade; they're actually moving in the opposite direction.

"The world's preoccupation with authenticity is being diluted by its curious experiments with deepfake – sometimes usefully, sometimes viciously."

It's only fair to mention that, as soon as we discovered people were looking for 'authenticity', we managed to manipulate it to the point where even authenticity started to look fake. A feat that only advertising and marketing experts can achieve. We can probably be credited with priming our audience to be perfectly comfortable with fake. Social media platform algorithms are also to blame for templating what it takes to win over a large number of people. If deepfakes can help with that, authenticity can take a backseat.

But now we have a new maze to navigate. We need to rewire our instinct to believe everything we see. To be technically precise, we now need to learn not to believe what we see. 'Seeing is believing' used to be sufficient evidence, which is why that idiom has been in use for centuries. Now, suddenly, 'seeing is disbelieving.'

The era in which fame is comparatively easily accessible is also the era where it is safest to remain completely unknown. The era in which information is most easily spread is also the era in which it is hardest to combat the wildfire of misinformation. Audio and video evidence no longer carry the weight they once did. Until effective fake-detectors are developed, people in videos and audios will need to be granted the benefit of the doubt—or the liar's dividend.

There have been instances where people transferred money to a friend after a phone call with the friend, only to realize it was a scam using the exact voice of the friend. There have been several incidents of deepfake misuse, including destruction of reputation, blackmail, and misinformation. Like with all new inventions, generative AI has a dark side but can also be used for great good. Deepfake technology is proving useful in many disciplines, such as education and training, and even in unexpected places, such as protecting the identities of people in documentary films. All is not bleak.

There are companies dedicated to developing technologies that help us distinguish between the fake and the real, enabling us to protect ourselves. One thing is for certain: deepfakes will impact the way we perceive the world in unimaginable ways.

As brand strategists, we must think about ways to incorporate heightened avenues for building trust in real life (IRL) via multiple sources of information and content into our brand-building strategies.

POOJA NAIR

Trust Is A Tough Puzzle

CHAPTER XIX

Compromised Privacy

When they said even the walls have ears, they didn't mean it in absolute terms. Information doesn't always travel through walls. In the same way, experiments on smart phones to test if they are listening to our conversations have not yielded consistent results for us to conclude that phones indeed listen to us, all of the time. At least not without our permission. Of course, when we start with "Hey Siri," "Hello Google," the phone is designed to listen to us, and we are aware of this.

What we also know, is that even without listening per se, our activities on our phones provide legitimate access to more data about us than we can imagine. Our likes and dislikes, where we travel, what we buy, how we buy, how often we do it, our sleeping patterns, our health concerns, the people we love and in all possibility the people we dislike are just a few of the things our phones can be used to understand us better than the people who love us or live with us. Phones can also be used to ascertain who the other smartphone users are that we spend the most time with in physical proximity. Point being, they have enough data on us without needing to also listen to us clandestinely.

Question is whether this is creepy or useful for us? Personally, I like that if I am looking to purchase running shoes, I see all kinds of options for running shoes. Problem is I still see those ads even after I have purchased the shoes. So much for having real-time data about me!

Whether we like it or not, it doesn't look like we will be able to escape having to adjust to compromised privacy.

However, there are ways to control it. We can adjust how much our phone listens to us by taking the effort to go onto 'settings' and look into each app and switch off audio permissions. However, when we do that, it compromises our experience of the app. For instance, we won't be able to send voice texts. Voice messaging has been a boon to people who don't enjoy typing or are not comfortable with English. Voice texts also help convey things with lesser chances of misunderstandings caused by the open-to-interpretation tone of voice in plain texts. But to be able to use voice text we need to give the app the permission to use the phone mic.

So yes, we risk losing our privacy. But is this any more a matter of concern than eavesdropping neighbours and well, walls? The latter could sometimes be far bigger threat. It's all relative, of course. It remains to be seen if in the years to come, technology as well as humans will evolve in such a way that helps us have a better grip on 'privacy control'.

> *"One option of course is to switch to feature phones. Feature phones allow us to be contactable while preventing apps from using us (data about us). Or us from using apps."*

Quick service apps like Swiggy and Blinkit, on-demand taxi services like Rapido and Namma Yatri, the one and only Google Maps etc are all great inventions but it seems unfair that to be able to benefit from them, we have to adjust to our privacy being compromised and dealing with the anxiety of being listened to and all our movements being carefully recorded and analysed. But if we think about it in this way that it is all used to serve us better or advertise to us, more relevantly, and not to judge us and gossip like eavesdropping neighbors are notorious for, it may be seen as a consolation.

Privacy as a concept is changing. In the years to come, humanity may indeed adjust mindsets to cope with this price it pays for a fantastically more convenient and better-served living. Meanwhile, we need to do as much to alleviate consumer anxiety around this as possible.

Nosy Smartphones

CHAPTER XX

Self-Defence In The Digital Age

Gone are the days when the most commonly feared petty crimes were chain snatching and burglary. With the rise of the Internet of Things, Web 3.0, and machine learning/ artificial intelligence, we now face a far more complex set of threats. Today, personal protection requires an understanding of technology. Whether it's for career advancement or safeguarding ourselves, we all need to grasp the basics of tech.

Self-defense has taken on a new meaning in this phygital world. Traditional martial arts or the ability to outrun an attacker won't be much use in the online universe. We need to learn about cookies—those small text files created and updated when we visit websites. These files help websites remember us and track our activities to provide personalized experiences. We must educate ourselves on password protection, how to delete browser histories, how to spot unknown callers and scam emails, and understand what makes our accounts vulnerable to hackers. We also need to be aware of photoshopped images designed to mislead, deepfake videos meant for deceit, and how to use fact-checking tools to determine what we should trust.

"Navigating crime in this big bad digitized world is becoming increasingly complex, but it is not impossible to understand."

The traditional art of pickpocketing has largely become obsolete in the face of modern crime. I recall seeing "beware of pickpockets" signs in crowded places when I was younger. Similarly, with proper awareness campaigns, we can reduce the risk of falling victim to cybercrime—not 100%, but to a significant extent. However, the increasing sophistication of these crimes keeps us in a constant battle.

Digital technologies serve as a tool that amplifies both our work and organized crime. As incidents of financial fraud, identity theft, job losses, and other crimes rise, people are becoming increasingly suspicious—both online and offline.

There are four key cyber threats to watch out for:

Hacking: Gaining unauthorized access to a computer system or account.

Phishing: Impersonating legitimate companies or individuals to trick users into revealing sensitive information.

Malware: Spreading malicious software, including viruses, worms, trojans, and ransomware.

Identity Theft: Stealing personal data to fraudulently assume someone's identity.

But perhaps the most insulting of all crimes are those conducted through mere phone calls. In these scams, uninformed victims are convinced to willingly disclose personal information, scan barcodes, or download malicious apps. Unfortunately, there is little cyber police can do when customers willingly hand over their data, despite the losses they face.

In the coming years, as we begin to better understand how to work with generative AI and Answer Engine Optimization (AEO), we must also focus on improving our collective awareness of cybersecurity to protect ourselves from political, financial, and other online crimes. Just as in real life, we are always vulnerable to risks in the virtual world, but there are plenty of measures we can take to protect ourselves.

Any brand, regardless of its category, can play a role in helping people better manage their cybersecurity. The war on cybercrime is real, and brands that empower individuals to arm themselves with the right knowledge will earn a stronger connection with their audience.

Self-Defence In The Digital Age

WHAT'S NEXT?

CHAPTER XXI

Gen Alpha, Growing Up Fast

Here's a fun fact. Generation X was named after Author Douglas Coupland's 1991 novel, Generation X: Tales for an Accelerated Culture. Consequently, the following generations were dubbed, Gen Y and Gen Z. Taking us back to the beginning of the alphabet for the next generation. This seems symbolic of the impact this generation is poised to have on the culture of the world. A re-start. A do-over.

The first generation to not know of a world without social networking. The generation that sees social media as a career. The generation that sees the 2014 aesthetic as vintage. Gen Z YouTuber, Haylo Hayley feels old as she rants about this in one of her vlogs. That's right. Gen Alpha is already making Gen Zers feel old.

The internet hit the scene in the late 90s, mobile phones soon after, mobile phones with internet a little after that, and then social media apps and now, gulp, generative AI. Every generation misses simpler times. Same holds true for Gen Z. They miss the times where they could post on social media without the reflection of ring-lighting in their eyes. Gen Alpha is occupied by an online world and their avatars in them. They are too distracted to read. But that, by no stretch, means they are less informed. They are not innocent about the scams, crimes, wars, discrimination, and ecological damage that is happening today. They are in touch with reality like no previous generation was at their age. For the generation that experienced the pandemic in their formative years, the only way to survive is to keep things labsurd. (More on this in the next chapter.)

Conversely, they are victims of the universal human traits of this stage of physical development. This is the awkward age when they first start exploring self-identity, experience soaring passions, and earth-shattering heartbreaks. The chief source of validation for this generation happens to be social media where they are being fed with rigid notions on what's cool and what's not in fashion and with unheard of measures of body perfection such as calf size and the ideal angle between the nose and the upper lip.

The same social media platforms that provided millennials and Gen Zers a means to explore and constantly reinvent their individuality are boxing Gen Alpha with algorithms for vanity metrics. This has given birth to 'influencer schools' to teach people how to go viral. These schools essentially hand out a set formula to become an influencer which is a legit career option now.

Gen Alpha is only about 12 when generative AI has entered the arena. They will own the intelligence of AI by the time they form the workforce. Nobody older than them is as equipped to take charge of the world that is to come. Not after we are gone but much before that. It may be apt to say that our collective future lies in the hands of Generation Alpha.

> *"But today, they are also just children at an awkward age who need to be protected from the tyranny of social media validation."*

We, along with Generation Alpha, need to together carve out a way to benefit from our online existence and not be destroyed by it. Earlier we protected our children from the real world. Now we also protect them from the online world. Some things remain the same.

To get Gen Alpha, we need to listen, observe, and hope to learn because, after all, they are the first generation born in this suddenly changed world.

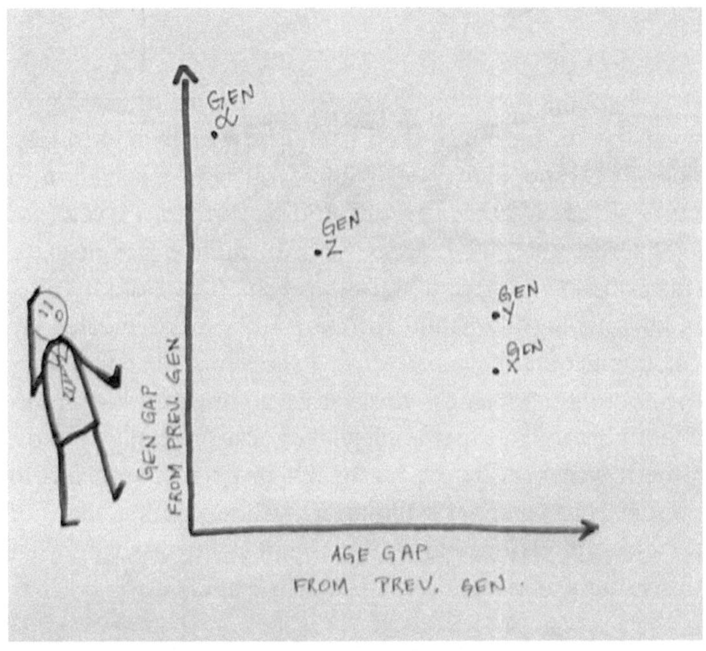

Please Mind The Gap

CHAPTER XXII

Gaming World Fuses Into The Real World

If the youngest members of society are an indication of what the future holds, then it will be worthwhile to take note of the popularity of Skibidi Toilet. If reports are to be believed, it is a rage with kids less than 14 years of age, across the globe. More than 38 million people have subscribed to it since it started in Feb 2023. Skibidi Toilet is an ongoing animated YouTube web series created by Georgian content creator Alexey Gerasimov. The nature of the content is causing a moral scare among grown-up folks about how the internet is allegedly poisoning young minds. Whether these fears are reasonable or extreme remains to be seen, but what we can't ignore is how gaming codes of tonality, animation, sound effects and attitudes shape what this audience finds enjoyable IRL (in real life).

"Video games seem to have birthed a new generation that is completely desensitised to what people so far found absurd, violent or absurdly violent."

From consoles to PCs to mobiles, gaming has made quite a journey, getting more and more sophisticated in storylines and imaginative in characters. Gaming went from being a mere source of amusement to becoming a serious spectator sport to impacting pop culture. Not all video games are violent or absurd. CandyCrush is a video game too. A differently absurd game, some may argue. No matter the nature of the game, its sound effects have a distinct trait that can be recognised as 'gaming' sounds. The pixelated, animated and exaggerated characters of video games are unmistakable. Video games imitated real life in its own limited ways and provided an escape into a world of fantasy. In the last few years, the opposite began to happen.

"The real world started imitating the world of video games, erasing the lines between fantasy and real."

Younger people whose lives are equal parts real and virtual from the time they were born, seem to be immune to the artificialness of the virtual world. They perhaps see no divide between the real and the virtual or don't view the divide the way we grown-ups do. The virtual doesn't just seem real, the virtual is real. In their reality.

A few years ago, I stumbled on the phenomena of 'cosplay' – a means of expressing fandom where fans dress up as certain characters from video games, or Manga, or any show they like. Cosplayers are known for their versatility and strong attention to detail, combining the skills of sewing, foam and thermoplastic work, prop building, wig styling, special effects makeup and more into their work to ensure everything looks according to a specific character's design. Popular cosplay influencers in their LIVE streams emoji-react every time a user sends them a reaction. This, to put it simply, is real people mimicking the imperfections of CG creations to perfection. The world seems to be turning upside down. But to the next generation of society, all this seems in the right order.

Video games are even influencing fashion. In early 2024, Tommy Hilfiger teamed up with games publisher Tilting

Point to create its own fashion styling game, called FashionVerse. Brands are recognising the potential of the gaming industry to connect with people in an immersive way and foster stronger connections with their amphibian customers - breathing equally at ease in the real and gaming world.

Like most things, video games have the good, the bad and the ugly side to it, but it is a force to reckon with. The gaming ecosystem is an unmistakable way to build a community to bond with customers as a brand - today and in the times to come.

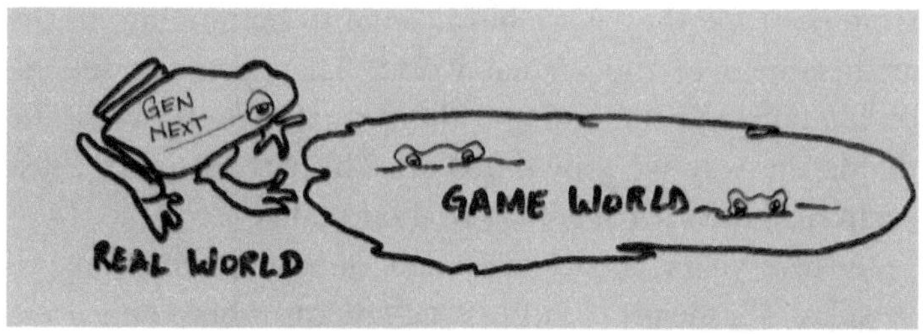

Gen Next - At Home In Both Habitats

CHAPTER XXIII

Avatars – 'Fact Is Stranger Than Sci-fi'

If we want to learn to be able to converse with anyone in the world, we will need to learn how to do it in 7151 ways. That's the number of recognised spoken languages in the world, according to the World Atlas Society. Not just words, but even gestures can have different meanings in different regions. The thumbs-up sign, which is recognised as a sign to wish somebody the best, also means 'thenga' – a North Indian way of referring to 'nothing'. Having said that, there is a universal language that connects humans across geographies. Everyone understands a smile. Human conversations are nothing without these expressions and body language. This is why, when our conversations moved to online chat windows, we started using emoticons created using punctuation marks and alphabets. They worked much better than typing out the words, "I am smiling" or "I am winking."

Way back in 1982, Professor Scott Fahlman, a computer scientist at Carnegie Mellon University, used the first digital emoticon. And it was a smiley face. :) Have you noticed how the nature of emoticons people use can give away their age, in most cases? If they are fond of making a 'tongue out smiley' with a colon and small letter 'p', in all chances they are in their late 30s or older. :p

The first emoji were created in 1999 by Japanese artist Shigetaka Kurita for Docomo. Emoji is a Japanese word that translates in English as 'e' for 'picture' and 'moji' for 'character'. Kurita's original 176 emoji are now part of the permanent collection at New York's Museum of Modern Art. They vastly improved our ability to add emotional subtext to our texts while conversing online with symbols like the heart or a bolt of lightning. As mobile conversations exploded, companies outside Japan, like Apple, saw an opportunity to incorporate emoji on other platforms. In 2007, a team at Google decided to petition to get emoji recognised by the Unicode Consortium, a non-profit group that works to maintain text standards across computers. Emoticons and emojis, together, help us fill the void created by online conversations. In addition, they helped foster a universal language, more or less, for humans across borders. There are exceptions, of course, such as the 'high-ten' emoji being happily used as a 'namaste' by Indians.

Today, the tussle between our offline and online existence has taken on a whole new dimension. If our earlier preoccupation was about bringing alive our bodily expressions in virtual conversations, then now it is about not being limited by our bodies at all. We are inventing ways to travel through time, cultures and distances instantly, unrestricted by our physical form and circumstances. With many selves, we can be at multiple places at once. This could sound unsettling and exciting at the same time. It does sound like it is the premise of a sci-fi movie. But avatars are real.

Avatars hold potential to evolve into something more dynamic in the not-so-distant future. Avatar, a term with Sanskrit origins, technically means "an incarnation, embodiment, or manifestation of a person or idea". But in the digital space, we generally understand them as the little cartoon person we create to represent ourselves in video games, on social media, or on web forums.

According to head of Instagram Adam Mosseri, *"Avatars are a key building block for the future of personal identity in the metaverse."* Slowly but surely, we are witnessing a growing number of avatar reactions to our posts, stories, reels and chat messages instead of emojis. Sooner or later, we may all need to, or even want to, get on the bandwagon.

> *"Our avatars need not be consistent with our physical attributes in real life, enabling us to explore possibilities of who we want to be without the limitations of our offline being. Be yourself or escape yourself. We have the choice."*

As the metaverse becomes an increasingly immersive place for humans to hang out, work, trade, play and socialise, avatars become the form in which we exist in it. Avatars will forge the reality we choose for ourselves in the virtual universe running parallel to our actual universe.

The challenge for brands will become defining our TG persona. If the persona is multi-faceted with many avatars, we will need to identify underlying universal truths of the metaverse culture to tap into instead.

Be Yourself Or Escape Yourself

CHAPTER XXIV

Metaverse Culture

The search for signs of life on other planets could still take time. Meanwhile, we have created a parallel universe right here on Earth, which is up and functioning, enabling us to be at multiple locations at the same time. 'Sci-fi max!' as my Gen Z friends may remark. Except that this is sci-fact.

A phenomenal shift in human existence is underway and is bringing along with it a host of transformations in the way we operate:

Crafting to Generating – In the physical world, we take pride in craftsmanship – be it when crafting a tagline for a brand, weaving a carpet, or sculpting forms out of rock. In the metaverse, craftsmanship takes a back seat. When machines replaced manual labour, it may have caused the same dissonance at first. To this day, anything that is hand-crafted holds a premium over anything machine-made, even if they look identical to the ordinary eye. Perhaps items crafted in the real world will demand a similar premium over items generated using AI. But, we are moving to a generation-dominant ecosystem.

Competition to Collaboration – The universe has been expanding ever since the Big Bang, but earthlings are still limited to and by Earth for survival, at least so far. The metaverse, on the other hand, eliminates the limitations caused by a depletion of resources. There is no scarcity here. There is room for everyone and everything. This saves people the need to race one another and allows them to focus on output together. The abundance mindset is creating a society of self-assured, self-caring people who believe in building each other up. 'Neighbour's envy' will be passé. (Ref: Indian television ad for Onida TV from the 80s)

Teaching to Facilitating – To quote a part of a Sanskrit mantra, 'guru brahma, guru vishnu, guru devo maheshwara' – the teacher is Brahma, the teacher is Vishnu, the teacher is Maheshwara. Ancient civilisations understood the value of what teachers offer society. That hasn't changed. What has changed is that education can now be accessed easily and repeatedly by knowledge seekers at their convenience, from any part of the world. We can pick and choose where and how we learn. Teachers are voluntarily stepping down from their pedestal. They facilitate, guide, and coach from a peer position. Facilitating individual pursuits of self-potential exploration may be a good way for brands to vibe better.

Action First, Perfection Later – Earlier, every hasty camera click meant wasted film roll. Every error in the printed form meant printing out or buying a fresh form. Missing a turn on the road could mean being completely lost without any idea of the way to get back on track. Ads with slightly wrong details or tonality or media planning incurred heavy penalties. Today, we can and need to keep iterating our ads every day. The mantra of the day seems to be to go for it and learn through doing, instead of getting it perfect first. Just like LLMs (large language models), our learning too will tend to happen and grow as we keep working. Quantity over quality of messages heightens the chances of the best quality of communication through constant testing, analysis, and iteration.

Fitting-in to Finding-what-fits – In the virtual universe, there are no set templates of right and wrong or beautiful and ugly, or funny and boring or cool and uncool. There is an audience for everything. We can keep on reinventing ourselves until we find our audience. Yes, it is a troll-happy place, but it is as much a place full of supporters. Malayalam actress Lena was trolled heavily for sharing about her exceptional memory, including that of her previous birth on Earth. She did not care. She found it amusing. This attention led her to find a publisher for her own book and also meet her now-husband. People are comfortable owning who they are. A tricky situation for brands that fed off customer insecurities. New-age brand builders are orienting themselves towards working around customer self-worth.

He-man to Femme-power – The masters of the virtual universe are all about acceptance of pansexual identity, with a definite admiration for female attributes. In the metaverse, He-Man's cat can embrace its identity of Cringer Cat and Battle Cat both with equal pride. Patriarchy is not going down alone. It is taking with it gender prejudice, unnecessary machismo, notions of damsels in distress, unquestioned authoritarianism, gaslighting, and snobbery in general. To be taken seriously in this new world, we need to dial up empathy, sensitivity, jokes that punch-up, not down, and see the strength in softer traits of nurture and kindness.

With conventional indicators of age, gender, geography, and education being susceptible to fluidity, TG (target group) profiling may need to be based more on mindsets, attitudes, and culture.

Metaverse Etiquette

CHAPTER XXV

Intangible Money

Once upon a time, cocoa beans and peppercorns were known to have been used as currency for the high value they held. Today, something invisible has taken that role: money you can't see or touch. Let's hear an applause for digital currency! Also called digital money or cybercash, it refers to currency that is available only in digital or electronic form. It has utility similar to physical currency and can be used to purchase goods and services. It can also find restricted use among certain online communities, such as gaming sites, gambling portals, or social media networks. Digital currencies are particularly useful for instant transactions seamlessly executed across borders.

Are we heading for a synthetic, robotic world, devoid of human physical contact, with each one lost in their respective cyber cloud? Will we be familiar with only the avatars of people? Will we ourselves be in touch with our avatars more than our real selves? The answers, my friend, are blowing in the wind. The scenario we are heading towards seems to be cold and unearthly. But wait. What about the increasing acceptance of the sexuality spectrum? The growth in mental health awareness? The never-before emphasis on teaching empathy and kindness in school curriculums? The explosion of career possibilities? The platform for the previously powerless and voiceless to express their points of view and art sans gatekeepers? Education being accessible across every corner of the world? And along the same lines, money and financial services being accessible across geographies, urban and rural? There's lots of warm humaneness too.

The digitisation of money may just catalyse our collective shift towards a society that aims to provide equal opportunity to all classes, genders, races, and ethnicities, irrespective of what government election results in major markets look like. Digital currency also provides a fairer system for people with disabilities and mobility restrictions. To balance out the utopian nature of these possibilities is the increased sophistication of cybercrime. Technological adoption to be able to make the most of digital money and understanding cyber security are two sides of the same coin.

The digitisation of currency robs us of the satisfaction of touching and counting out our money, or the cheap thrill of mimicking movie moments of throwing bundles in the air with an evil laugh. Okay, nobody does that for real. But now we know we can't if we wanted to.

> *"Intangible money may feel dystopian for the loss of familiarity, but it holds potential to make money easier for all sections of the population."*

Banks are intimidating for a large portion of society. Digital ownership and transactions heighten the chances of unbiased dignity when availing financial services.

There are three types of digital currencies, namely, cryptocurrencies, virtual currencies, and central bank digital currencies (CBDC). All cryptocurrencies are digital currencies, but not all digital currencies are cryptocurrencies. The key characteristic of all digital currency is that they do not have any physical form, although they may be exchanged for physical money or other assets.

As per AtlanticCouncil.org, as of September 2024, 134 countries and currency unions representing 98% of the global GDP are exploring CBDC. Every G20 country is exploring a CBDC, with 19 of them in the advanced stages of CBDC exploration. Of those, 13 countries are already in the pilot stage. This includes Brazil, Japan, India, Australia, Russia, and Turkey. Three countries have fully launched a CBDC—the Bahamas, Jamaica, and Nigeria.

We need to evaluate the impact such a shift can have on behaviour and attitudes towards money and wealth creation, TG profiling, how and when we buy things, and consequently on brand choice.

Intangible Money

CHAPTER XXVI

Trust Will Follow Thorough Verification

There was a time just over 20 years ago when news was presented in a neutral tone 2–4 times a day on TV and radio. Be it on print, radio, or TV, 'the daily news' had its own weight in gold because it was something a journalist reported. Those were the days when these deliverers of news were trusted and feared by the mightiest in society.

Then, someone thought up 24-hour news channels. More money could be made that way. It may cause a minor setback to news as a concept. But, more money can be made that way. Pretty soon, news degenerated into a form of entertainment and callous fictionalisation. Anything to keep the audience hooked for 24 hours, 7 days of the week. More money is made this way. In India, it has been at least 15 years since this shift started.

Yet, a considerable part of humanity, especially those born earlier than 30 years ago, are still conditioned to not question any bit of information presented to them as 'news'. Even a neatly formatted WhatsApp message is often swallowed without question.

Misinformation, brainwashing, and misunderstandings disguised as 'news' generated for personal profit have led to on-ground rioting, killings, and mass support for death and destruction. Things took a real ugly turn before the reliability associated with 'news sources' began to fade. Better late than never.

Everyone knows now that it has become easier to doctor videos and photographs than it is to slice bread. Biases are easy to feed into. Misleading news spreads easier than melted butter on those slices of bread. If it's any solace, technology is available for all of us to benefit from equally, not just malicious news generators. People, especially the younger demographic, enjoy the challenge of identifying whether something is real or fake.

There is a growing network of not-for-profit fact-checkers who are dedicating themselves to help people navigate harmful misinformation. The Poynter Institute for Media Studies is a non-profit journalism school and research organisation in St. Petersburg, Florida.

"The International Fact-Checking Network (IFCN) at Poynter was launched in 2015 to bring together the growing community of fact-checkers around the world."

They work towards the global fight against misinformation and support fact-checkers through networking, capacity building, and collaboration. IFCN's network reaches over 170 fact-checking organisations around the globe through advocacy, training, and events. Their team monitors trends in the fact-checking field to offer resources to fact-checkers, contribute to public discourse, and provide support for new projects and initiatives that advance accountability.

In India, since early 2013, FactChecker.in has been scrutinising and researching the veracity and context of statements made by individuals in public life, as well as picking up on issues that warrant an examination of data that is accessible to the public. On the same mission is

Boom, an independent digital journalism initiative in India. They explain issues and make the internet safer. Boom is certified by IFCN.

The phenomenon is not just restricted to the urban intellectual. Taking the initiative to small cities and villages is FactShala, formed with the support of the Google News Initiative. FactShala helps people across India critically evaluate news sources and sift facts from misinformation. They work with publishers and journalists to fight misinformation and share resources.

Several other organisations are geared up to stand with the growing number of people who seek to verify anything that is presented to them as news, and even more so, as 'breaking news'.

*Here's a 'fact check' for businesses and brand builders: people are just not going to remain as gullible as we had them before. **The future customer will demand advanced accountability.** The public is becoming able to discern advertising from outright drivel.*

Open-Eyed Trust

CHAPTER XXVII

Everyone, A 'Techie'

Until the late 90s, a typewriting course was something all students were advised to do on the side, towards the end of school or during graduation. Knowing how to type greatly improved your chances of finding employment.

My father had advised me against doing a typewriting course because he had the foresight to know that computers and their accompanying keyboards were going to change the way workplaces across domains would function and that typing would no longer be seen as a special skill. I saw his point and did not formally learn typewriting. Despite that, just as he anticipated, today I type at high speed, eyes on the screen, not on the keyboard.

Typewriting continues to be a basic skill. It's just that we happen to pick it up automatically, given the way a major part of our lives is spent on keyboards. There is another skill which is slowly turning into a similar life skill, but unlike typewriting, not automatically picked up. Yet.

Coding — something needed to make the most of the new world, which allows us to create apps or e-commerce-enabled websites at near-zero cost. Nearly everything now runs on digital technology and the only way to take advantage of, if not survive in, it is to learn at least the basic principles of programming code. Generative AI helps us with code, but even to be able to provide the right prompts, we need a working knowledge of programming languages.

The parallel online universe where we will exist as much as we do in the physical universe makes coding language comprehension a basic education parameter, as much as spoken language comprehension is, along with maths, science, and social studies. Whether or not we want to pursue a career in tech, just simple living will be smoother with an understanding of how coding works. If nothing else, it helps us develop problem-solving skills and gives wings to our ideas and creativity, irrespective of our professional domain.

> *"'Democratisation' is one of the overarching themes in this book. And still, I never thought I would say what I am about to say next. Today, software creation is democratised."*

Everybody can do it. It's become easy and convenient. Low-code and even no-code development platforms are on the rise. These allow people with even a basic level of coding expertise to build applications with minimal hand-coding.

The carpet is laid out for an exciting era of innovation and evolution with the active participation of people like you and me. By that, I mean people who categorise themselves as being non-tech. Knowing how to code greatly improves our chances of being of continued value to our employers and also for ourselves, no matter the discipline we work in.

> *Being non-tech will become akin to not knowing how to calculate percentages. Yes, many of us use calculators, but that's because we know how numbers work. The same applies here. While there's assisted programming, we will still need a basic understanding of how coding works to be able to use it right.*

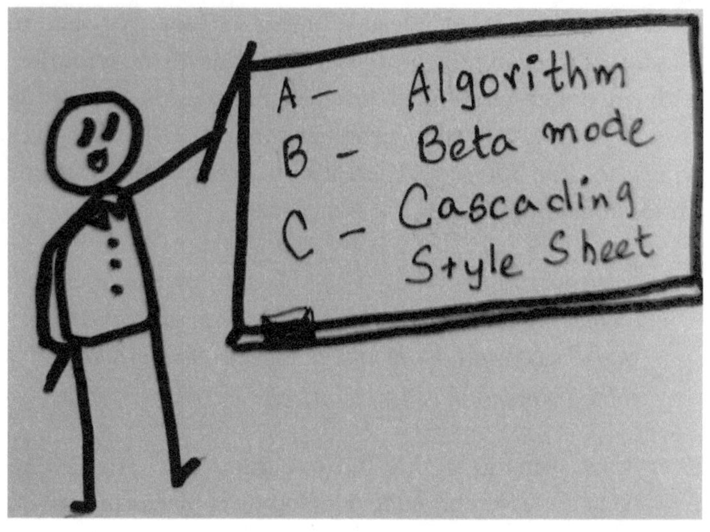

Everyone, A Techie

CHAPTER XXVIII

QR Codes – An Overlooked Boon

We may or may not be slow with technology, but technology keeps getting quicker. Not only are they at every online and offline location we go to, we will most likely find Quick Response (QR) codes hiding in every nook of our home too. They have sneaked into our cupboards, wallets and food. Most of the time, we simply ignore them. Yet, slowly and suddenly, QR scan codes have been pushing us towards tech-savviness, whether or not we are ready for it.

Thanks to situations where we are forced to learn to use them, such as for payment, at least in India, owing to India's homegrown digital payment systems, for their sheer superiority as a technology for financial transactions. No one is spared from it. From roadside sellers and bargain hunters to high-street salespeople and window shoppers. There are areas we can skirt using scan codes, such as at restaurants that are increasingly doing away with the physical menus altogether. Here some of us can just ask someone else at the table to scan the menu on their phone and read it out to us. Until we discover that the experience of accessing the menu on our own phone is much better. A discovery which takes that first spark of willingness to step outside of the familiar zone. But once people do, there's no looking back.

Comedian Samay Raina tweeted, *"If I ever get a tattoo, it will be of my UPI QR code."* It takes an openness to risk appearing foolish as we fumble through what many find as natural as breathing (or getting a tattoo). The rewards of enduring this humiliating phase to cross over to the world of scan codes is like taking the chance to step onto Aladdin's magic carpet – it can take you wonder by wonder over sideways and under. Refer to the lyrics of the song, 'A Whole New World' from Disney's Aladdin to get the picture. In the song, it is fantasy, but here it is real.

The utility of QR codes can go much beyond payment gateways. If we pay attention, we will see QR codes staring at us from everywhere. For most, they are blind spots. Unless marketers incentivise them well enough. Most of the things we buy today come with a QR code on the packaging. Except for discounts, most of us are unlikely to actually scan the code.

> "*We have the technology, but we are yet to juice the creative potential it holds to amplify our brand story and delight our audience. QR codes are power-packed with possibilities for brand building, advertising and marketing.*"

For the culturally inclined, at art museums, you may find a tiny scan code humbly placed on a corner of many of the exhibits. I seldom see visitors scan them to know more about the art. I did once at NGMA, National Gallery of Modern Art, Bangalore and it was a delightful revelation. My friend had simply assumed, *"I think the code is for when you want to share this exhibit on social media,"* she said. I didn't know what to expect either, but what I discovered was a fascinating story about the art, the artist and other trivia. It elevated my experience to another level. Ever since that incident, whenever I see a code, I get curious to see what it will unfold. Almost like a wrapped gift – no matter what is in it, the anticipation of what's inside is thrilling. What unfolds when I scan QR codes doesn't necessarily always match up to the anticipation. There you go! That's what brand strategists and creative professionals need to think of.

Give people something exciting to live up to the anticipation we feel when unwrapping a gift. Scanning the QR code should give scanners something beyond manufacture-speak about who we are and where we come from. They could be fun Easter eggs with trivia, a game, a story, a meme or a tool to enhance their next social media post. The shape and colour can be played with to align with the brand's identity. QR codes are incredibly versatile and can be adapted into various shapes without losing functionality.

QR codes are the glue between the physical and digital. Between online and offline advertising. What QR codes reveal need to be aligned with the brand ad campaign at any given point of time. Brand marketing heads along with their key advertising partners need to take on the responsibility of bringing QR codes to life as per brand guidelines.

QR Codes Can Save The Day

CHAPTER XXIX

The Intelligence That Will Count

The complexity of human intelligence is that it can be downright foolish. The intelligence in most other creatures is limited to mere instinct for survival and some playfulness with the assurance of no threat to their life. To say that the intelligence in humans is more advanced is an understatement. We have now manufactured a non-natural intelligence so sharp that it is threatening human intelligence itself—something our intelligence had many years ago already imagined. It may be seen as foolish for humans to create something that may threaten humanity. But this is not even the first time humans have done this. We are now habituated to inventing things that could potentially destroy humanity.

"That's human intelligence—ever fascinated with more intelligence, sometimes landing in lost intelligence."

Psychologist Howard Gardner, in his 1983 book Frames of Mind, broke down human intelligence into seven spheres, proposing that human intelligence cannot be captured by a single measure. Gardner suggests that the intelligence of our species is a combination, in varying degrees, of linguistic, musical, logical-mathematical, spatial, bodily-kinesthetic, interpersonal, and intrapersonal intelligence. The concept of social and emotional intelligence was later introduced in 1990 by psychologists Peter Salovey and John Mayer.

With artificial intelligence, its key superiority over natural intelligence, for now, seems to be speed. What would take one or a team of humans hours, weeks, or years, AI takes a few seconds or minutes. Speed is another concept that fascinates humans, for some reason. As soon as we master a skill, we want to see how fast we can do it. Sports championships are often all about speed after they are about skill—unless the skill itself is about how fast we can do it. Business success depends on speed, for some reason. How best and how fast we can deliver a product or a service. Quality trumps everything, but nothing compares to quality delivered fast. In fact, in the business world, I see people compromising on quality for speed and nobody minding it much either. Except the end consumer—but those guys are lambs. Not for long.

Humans know the value of patience but seldom apply it in the workings of the world. That's human intelligence for you. We have created an intelligence that can deliver information and analysis at a speed impossible to match by human capability. This is nudging a re-evaluation of human intelligence.

> *"We are now being forced to rewire how and for what we use our brains to thrive in the job market."*

As long as humans were dealing with humans, there was the leverage of human shortcomings. A facility that made us crank up our charm to make up for missed deadlines. Conversely, to demand consistent quality of output no matter the nature of input and even extract it by preying on the personal existence of the other. AI, on the other hand, only operates on pure, mechanical clarity. Ah! So this is what joy feels like. It will deliver, in what seems like supersonic speed, exactly what you prompt—with as many examples as possible. If a human service provider asked this much from their clients, they often risked being labelled as 'unintelligent' or worse, too lazy to use their own brains and expected to deliver anyway. How often have you, in the position of a client or a manager, said or thought this about others? I am sure you are saying it to ChatGPT too. Thankfully, ChatGPT doesn't rely on a sense of self-worth and validation to operate.

> *"As we discern human intelligence from machine intelligence, anything sans empathy, emotional understanding, and respect for fellow humans may not be considered intelligent at all, by 'human' standards."*

Would this, in turn, make humanity a differently intelligent race? One where anything but clear, empathetic communication skills would be considered useless by human standards? The answer, as Bob Dylan and many others after him famously sang, is blowing in the wind. When machines first made their entry and started to replace manual labour, there were similar concerns which carried on for at least a generation of skilled craftsmen. But today, we sit back and reap the benefits of machines in every walk of life. If history is a guide, one scenario would be that in less than a generation we will not be able to imagine a life without AI to augment what we do. In a bygone era, we were obsessed with what separates us from monkeys. In the future, it may all be about what separates us from machines.

The growing sophistication of non-human intelligence will perhaps motivate humans to sharpen faculties that isolate humans from machines. This means we will focus on nurturing our intelligence for empathy, kindness, and understanding humaneness. For every other kind of intelligence, we will have machines.

There Is No Artificial Empathy

CHAPTER XXX

Dating In The Future

A movie called *Her* was released in 2013. It is a science fiction film about a man who falls in love with his artificially intelligent mobile phone assistant. The film is set in a fictional scenario. It conjures up a time in which forming emotional attachements with and even dating AI assistants is normal. When I watched the film, just a decade ago, I remember finding the whole idea utterly outlandish. I was thankful that this was definitely not something I would witness in my lifetime. Today, I hear of it starting to happen, and I am only in my early 40s. The growing sophistication of AI-enabled virtual bots is already laying the groundwork for a generation of people who might form meaningful relationships with their AI companions.

Even though online dating has been around long enough to qualify as a key cultural marker of our times, it is still a discomfort zone for most. And so, dating apps like Bumble help users with prompts to set the tone going. Today, technology innovators are taking things a notch higher.

Rizz is internet slang for style, charm, or attractiveness and is also the name of an AI dating assistant that helps people open up on dating apps. Addressing a similar need is Yourmove.AI, an app and website that offers an AI dating profile generator and reviewer, among other services. We have all seen movies where the mediator or wingman becomes the boyfriend. The 1997 Bollywood movie, Yes Boss, comes to mind. Just saying, it is known to happen. I know of real-life cases too.

We love to imagine the most dystopian scenario of what is to come. I am guilty of it too, like when I watched Her less than a decade ago.

But, if we go by recent technological developments and the impact they have had on human lives, we will see that human connections always find a way to thrive, like green trees sprouting out of concrete.

We create ways to fortify emotional connections instead of compromising them. Such as the emergence of IRL (in real life) dating services such as the Pear Ring Social Experiment, I covered in the chapter titled 'smart fatigue'.

> *"I can see how an AI bot can make a perfect companion to humans, given their ability to listen and learn with each interaction – an area humans fail at miserably."*

It is a never-ending debate whether one can be mechanical about dating or not. When it comes to AI bots, until the day machines develop the intelligence for emotions, that debate is settled. Yes, one can. Will AI dating minimise heartbreak, and how useful can AI-assisted dating or AI dates be in fostering everlasting relationships and companionships is something that will unfold in the generations to follow.

Will this spell the end of loneliness? Well, did the constant stream of amusement and entertainment available to us on demand end boredom? Boredom still exists in a new mutant form. The same will perhaps be true for loneliness. It will take a new form. What a relief!

Future Cupid

CHAPTER XXXI

Taboo In The Future

What would you say are things considered to be taboo? Women staying out late partying? Women staying out late partying in 'revealing' clothes? Boys and girls cozying up to each other on park benches or on a metro train? The phrase 'work-life balance' in the office? Men wearing make-up? Heterosexual men wearing make-up? Self-love? Self-love despite flaws? Divorce? Divorce with no regret? Taboo makes for sparkling debates.

As an idea, taboo is like mercury at room temperature. It moves in the direction of changing mindsets and takes the shape of the times. Individuals and communities learn to navigate it, heating it to varying degrees of temperature. The debates on what is and is not taboo have always been influenced by each new generation opening our minds a little more. And yet, since time immemorial, the idea of taboo has had an unchanged hold on culture and society. But today, the intensity of the word taboo is being diluted and, as a concept, is slowly but surely being destroyed. If we call something taboo today, there is a likelihood of it being seen as a joke.

The preoccupation with taboo is being replaced with the idea of living our authentic selves without a care for judgment about our weight, our family, our baldness, our careers, our sexuality, our personalities. No marks for pointing out that the catalyst for this is social networks allowing humans from across the globe to bypass gatekeepers and connect directly and share information. People are championing and supporting ideas that appeal to them, outside rulebooks.

> *"Lines separating what is approved of and disapproved of have melted. Previously unutterable ideas such as 'gender fluidity' and, indeed, 'work-life balance' are on the table."*

We are living in times where two universes are running alongside, even in the real world. One universe is populated with people who seek subtle ways of favouring casteism, gender bias, racial/ethnic stereotypes, ageism, the freedom to be judgmental, and punching down in their 'jokes'. Running parallel to it is the universe populated with people advocating mental health, balance, kindness, self-love, and building each other up with no judgment. Which of these universes do you think will expand in the years to come? The universe that rewards sacrificing personal time, health, and space to massage the ego of demanding employers and clients while feeding reckless corporate greed? Or the universe that focuses on effort-to-output ratio to facilitate a work-life balance and personal space for employees and adopts sustainability practices to grow profits and brand love for the employer? It will be interesting to see in the years to come.

The story as of now is that people who live their lives on their own terms to escape mindless toxicity are no longer mere outliers. If we look inside organisations that are successful in terms of profits and customer acquisition, we may still come across high stress levels and a proactive lack of empathy. What has changed is that it is no longer taboo to want and demand work-life balance and reject working in such environments. Every last employee is searching for this, no matter where they may be employed. And every employer is either getting busy trying to provide this or working on devious ways to counter these 'troublemakers'.

"Despite the resistance from people who discount these shifts as something that can simply be ignored in order to carry on as usual, the rise of real people is real."

When we lift our heads from our work dashboards and look around, we will *see* that bringing our authentic, vulnerable selves to work and unabashedly working towards spending quality time with self and family while making a living has stopped being taboo.

Perhaps the only taboo for brands and businesses will be words and actions that keep them or push them into a corner of irrelevance.

The Friendly Ghost

SO, WHAT?

CHAPTER XXXII

The War On Interruptive Advertising

All businesses need to achieve today through advertising is to pique target group (TG) curiosity enough to make them search for more information about us online. The danger in being preoccupied with classical thinking is that we end up being over-indexed on 'grabbing' attention. Our ideation is skewed towards negotiating with audiences to not 'skip ad,' which, let's face it, was always a lost battle. This approach eats away into budgets and thinking - that could be better spent advertising to and thinking for those who already are interested in and are - figuratively speaking - *dying* for our product/brand. Today, we have the resources to find them and talk to exactly them.

Marketers and creative professionals who have recognized this find it less conflicting to keep their messaging simple, clean, informative, and most importantly, short.

"The new benchmark of creative advertising is the ability to make people want to google us within 10-15 seconds."

We live in a world with two kinds of companies: ones that advertise on "who we are" and "what makes us great" narratives and ones that focus on "what we do for you" and "how to reach/buy us easily" narratives. In a different time, the former held value, but in the easy-information, quick-service times of today, impressing is no use unless accompanied by tons of content that is doing the job of informing and helping with today's audience's pursuit of post-purchase pride (ref chapter titled: 'post-purchase justification to post-purchase pride'). This means investing in impressive advertisements without a considerable investment and strategy on content covering reviews, buyer stories, user-generated testimonials, ideas, unboxing, and community management to name the basic list.

> *"Having advertising teams and content teams operate in their respective silos as separate profit centres hinders effective brand building."*

If we *see* the change in how we buy today, we will see that the role of advertising has changed from 'selling' to 'informing' those who are looking to make their choice. The 'selling' approach fundamentally involves manipulating consumer mindsets, which they can now catch.

> *"The 'informing' approach involves understanding consumer needs and providing assurance in their decision-making process. The latter needs a greater, if not the same, focus on content strategy as on the advertising campaign strategy—and for best results, should be tackled by the same team of brand strategists and creative professionals."*

Given that content needs a lot more thought and strategy in current times, it is a lot easier for content companies to take on the advertisement campaign strategy duties as well. From what I see, traditional advertising agencies often struggle with pandering to the *'veteran ego'* of millennial and older leaders. Moreover, an overhaul of decades-old organisational processes takes risky and bold decision-making, causing the oft-repeated in this book, resistance to change.

Coming back to the king - the consumer - the million-dollar question remains: what motivation would someone fully aware that they can search for anything they want at any time have to *not* skip an ad, no matter how entertaining and compelling it may be? The irony is that when we are searching for information on the very brand/product/service that interrupted us while we were watching/reading something else, we would again be interrupted by countless other brands that are not of interest in that moment. This, of course, is not entirely bad as it would at least mean those brands are targeting the viewer at a time when they are researching the product category.

Perhaps 'ads' and 'interruptions' will remain interchangeable as concepts. However, as brands, agencies, and companies, we now have a brilliant other way to connect with potential and existing customers.

> "*In the chaos of creating enrapturing interruptions, we must consider the equal, if not greater, importance of providing 'information' as and when needed. The team working on both needs to be consistent. Brand building is compromised without consistency.*"

Conventionally, we are also attached to the skill of telling brand stories in 30 secs or more. But the truth which has been hitting us in the face for a while now is that we need to be able to do it in half that time.

> "*Moreover, today, there is no reason to tell a story without providing a means for our audience to*

engage with us. "

It will be a matter of time before we acknowledge that almost no one ever actively opts to 'not skip' ads—not when they are playing games, not when they are browsing apps, not when they are reading news online, not when they are watching YouTube videos. Only when they are listening to Spotify, is it hard to skip ads because they may be away from the phone or have their hands busy with something else while listening. (more on this in the chapter titled: attention-grabbing to attention-worthy). Other than with audio ads, all signs point to the fact that advertisements are metamorphosing from interruptions to information and engagement for the customers looking for us.

Advertisements today take a different orientation of creativity. Ads per se need to tell the story in 15 secs or less. Other avenues such as podcasts, YouTube review videos, product unboxing, community engagement avenues, and verified user testimonial videos are the means to tell stories any longer than that aimed for those who googled us possibly after seeing the 15-sec ad

Chasing The Disinterested = Ignoring The Interested

CHAPTER XXXIII

The Emergence Of A Counter Ad Business Culture

Counterculture is the term given to the culture of rejecting or questioning dominant norms and conventions for value systems that seem completely radical and scandalous. The term counterculture first picked up in the '60s. It stirred thought and resistance by advocating fearless experimentation, inclusion, acceptance, and breaking away from the divides and chains that segregate and limit us. Cut to 60 years later, these are ideas that no longer sound bizarre. And yet, the fear of them lives on. This holds true for the discipline of marketing and advertising as well.

Brands predominantly have drawn from and, in turn, further fuelled mainstream culture. Representations of the ideal family, the ideal student, the ideal home, and ideal beauty were based on mainstream audience aspirations and mindsets. Sexism and objectification also, of course, are mainstream, and brands did not shy away from leveraging and, in turn, further magnifying it. When counterculture ideas began to gain prominence among the public, giant brands often looked the other way, preferring to continue mirroring mainstream motivations and aspirations, providing challenger and start-up brands with a nice, big elephant in the room to ride. Brands that stood for counterculture began to garner a share of the pie. Understandably, giant established brands tend to be afraid to touch counterculture simply because they have too much at stake. Also, the dominant value system is where the numbers are, at the end of the day. Or is it? The declining shares of some giant brands, are adding up to a new reality.

Testimony to this are brands that have stayed in tune with the times and dared to embrace countercultural nuances effectively - to emerge as the most popular among an evolving population. Previously inauspicious ideas of a second marriage were boldly represented by Tanishq jewellers 1.5 decades ago at a time when leading jewellery brands or any brand for that matter would not touch that idea, even though second marriages in urban India were on the rise. Winning the hearts of generations to come as daughters in urban India grow more and more involved in their wedding decisions. Another example is that of a still severely frowned-upon idea of live-in couples being represented by Red Label tea. The ad's depiction of how young adults and their parents have a strong inclination to eliminate the generation gap was as perfect as the cup of tea the brand promises. Dove's smashing of unrealistic beauty standards began in the U.S. as early as 2004 – a bold move that is continuing to help Dove stay relevant in the day of AI-manipulated videos. Laundry ads still depict soiled clothes as the prime headache of women alone. Ariel took a stand with the *'share the load'* campaign, owning a share of consumer love for generations to come. Nike deviated from showcasing professional athletes to include anyone who is willing to self-motivate to start their fitness journey, reflecting the brand's acknowledgement of the growing culture of sports and fitness among non-athletes. The list runs long.

> *"The use of counterculture to connect with consumers is not new to advertising. What is new is that the culture of advertising itself is being*

demolished as a counterculture style of the business is replacing it. **"**

The very foundational textbooks on advertising and branding will be re-written. Attempts to 'create needs' and force aspirations no longer work as well as they once did. No amount of celebrity endorsement can combat poor online reviews from peers. Even a complete lack of online reviews, for that matter, is sus (suspicious in Gen Z slang). Brands that don't take a stand on matters that matter at all pale before all the brands that do. Brands that don't live out the stand they take are called out. Ad scripts need to be able to tell the story in 15 secs. This demands clarity and prioritising of messaging. And the need to seamlessly work along with all other content initiatives.

Advertising and digital marketing professionals will perhaps continue to see each other as antagonists for as long as 'veteran' people with old-school mindsets run advertising businesses. In the next few years, as Gen Zers and Gen Z-minded folks start to run advertising businesses, the shape of advertising as a concept will finally undergo the change that the times warrant. Advertising = brand ads (15 secs) + on-brand content. Stitched together by the same team of strategists, client expectation managers and creative prefessionals. This whole system has to come under one roof, speaking the same language, using the same jargon. The entire team will identify as being creative techies.

Whether it will be content agencies that will rise to the occasion or whether it will be ad agencies that transform, or both, will be interesting to see. Perhaps a new crop of new-wave, counter-culture ad agencies will emerge. There definitely is a pressing need for it.

New Books Will Be Written For the Digital Age

CHAPTER XXXIV

Tackling Anti-Marketing

Not to dampen the sense of accomplishment of those of us who are beginning to get the hang of influencer marketing, but it looks like these trend-setters seem to be going off-trend—or are changing into something else altogether. The consumer is at the centre of everything, including in making and breaking influencers. Influencers exploded onto the scene when they offered the audience exactly what they were craving: real, relatable, honest content. But, give it time, and we marketers tend to kill every goose that lays the golden egg.

Traditional brand marketers and advertisers simply viewed influencer marketing as a direct replacement for TV commercials with controlled scripts and product placements. This created a void all over again where refreshing, unique content once stood.

Making way for a new phenomenon - de-influencing. De-influencers are social media users who discourage their followers from buying certain products and brands. When influencers came on the scene, they fulfilled a need-gap for truthful content. De-influencers have emerged to fill the gaping void created by a lack of truth in brand labelling, marketing, and advertising.

De-influencers focus on fact-checking, promote critical thinking, debunk misinformation, advocate for ethical consumerism, educate about media literacy, support social justice causes, and use humour to critique influencer culture. They empower their audience to question and engage with social media content responsibly.

Well-established brands have had to succumb to the pressure of de-influencing and carry out product composition or label changes. While these steps may control some of the damage, they may do little to counter the effects of being exposed among Indian consumers who have trusted these brands for generations.

> *"Until recent times, advertisers and marketers only needed to worry about finding loopholes in regulatory laws. Now, with consumers turning into vigilant hawks, we are being forced to be **actually truthful about claimed consumer benefits.**"*

The benefit could be simply a guilty indulgence. On the right occasions, there is lots to benefit from that too. But, we need to call it what it is.

This wave of anti-marketing need not spell doom for brands. Like any culture code, this one too can be leveraged by brands to connect with consumers better. In 2022, Dove turned into a de-influencer themselves with the #detoxyourfeed campaign in the U.S. to counter influencers flooding the internet with toxic beauty advice that ends up worsening self-image issues in vulnerable scrollers. For Dove, this builds on their two-decade-old brand purpose of tackling self-esteem concerns while effectively staying relevant to evolving consumer needs.

De-influencers are also influencers of a kind, just that they support truth at any cost. Influencers such as @MasalaLab urge their followers to question popular notions when making brand and diet choices.

> *"What we need to **see** is this: the era of the knowledgeable consumer has begun."*

There are going to be fewer and fewer possibilities of fooling them with age-old misleading tricks. Consumers can discern truth and intent in advertising from just advertising.

Brands need to advertise to people with truth and realness of intent. It is perhaps also time for companies to go beyond mere corrective measures in advertising and begin re-looking at the entire value chain through the lens of an informed and enabled consumer.

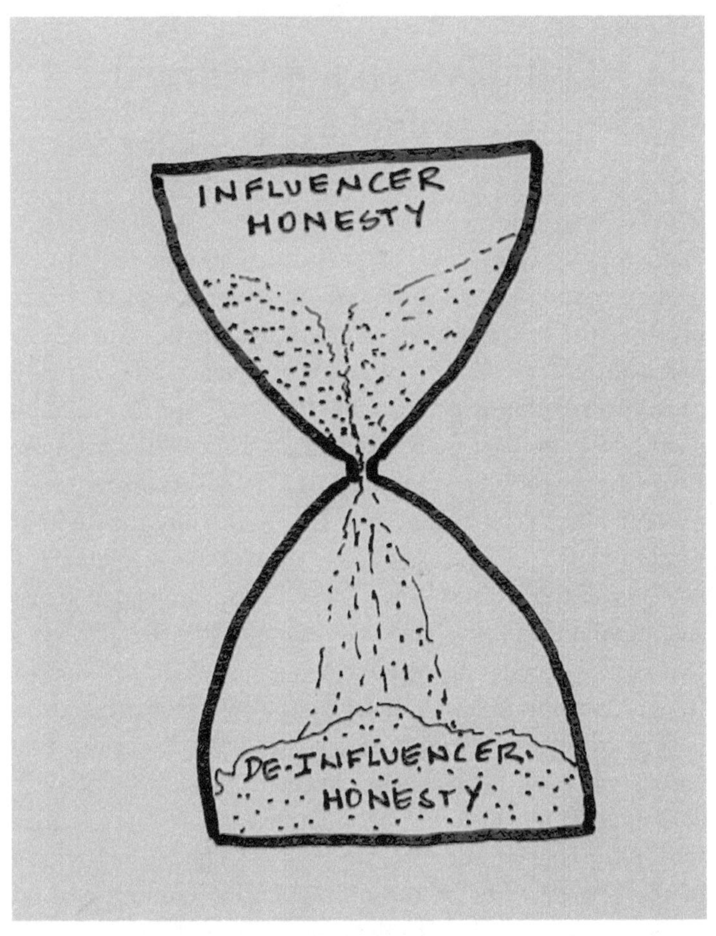

Advancing Demand for Advanced Accountability

CHAPTER XXXV

Brand Perception To Brand Reputation

I am a product of over 18 years of mainline advertising agency experience. However, in the last 3–4 years especially, I felt the need to move away from that scene just a little to be able to proactively unlearn and formally reskill to keep up with the changing landscape. More often than not, I was met with resistance within the ad agencies I worked at when I put forward new-world strategies, even though clients expressed the need for thinking in that direction.

This is the reason why, 2 years ago, I decided to go independent. This was the only way available to me to keep my practice relevant. We have been saying '360-degree integration' for at least 2 decades now, but true integration is something only dreams are made of. This is not due to a lack of willingness to integrate. It seems to be more because each communication vertical operates as a separate entity within the larger entity. We struggle to let go of the baggage of treating ad films as the only mainline communication while everything else is relegated to being below-the-line (BTL) advertising.

Shockingly, this resistance from ad agencies and traditional brand marketing teams did not stop the marketplace from turning on its head anyway. Today, brand stories are built not just through ad films but through content strategies. Content strategies effectively create an omnipresent effect for brands, making them accessible quicker, easier, and on the go. The touchpoints for ads and the point of purchase have been soldered together to become one and the same. This radically changes the purchase journey that traditional advertising agency personnel got too comfortable serving. The call for a radical shift in how we view branding and communication strategies has reached blaring levels.

It is traditional advertising and marketing's own doing that has caused consumer apprehension towards advertisements. Now, with the transfer of power into their own hands, people no longer need to worry about ads pulling the wool over their eyes. Be it on Google, social media communities, podcasts, blogs, or YouTube, customers seek out brands with honesty of intent and actual value to offer.

In the new world order, classic ad films are indeed turning into BTL with the sole role of driving awareness and curiosity. For everything else—from brand image building, forging meaningful consumer connections, creating an advantage over the competition, converting positive perceptions to sales—we rely on content strategies and digital marketing.

> *"There is a shift in client ask from ad scripts to content ideas tailored to various content platforms while also being on-brand—something people yet to let go of their classic ad-thinking hats struggle with."*

Brand preference is no longer influenced by ads alone. It is by the vibe the brand gives out, even in the news people hear about the brand—as employers, as manufacturers, and as value creators for customers and clients.

"Companies can no longer ignore the impact of their reputation, as audience attention increasingly shifts away from what is advertised to pretty much everything else about the company."

Today, customers are co-writing brand stories along with the brand 'custodians'. Through their own research, hashtags, reels, stories, and reviews, they are actively engaging with brands. This gives brands the chance to incorporate into brand strategy ways to make people feel like a part of the brand story and thereby feel a sense of ownership and affinity for it. A good example is Lego getting suggestions from its fan communities, getting them to vote, and then releasing sets with the most fan votes. This, along with several other initiatives, builds the brand's reputation as being true enablers for Lego builders. A perspective I gained from Prof. David Rogers during the digital marketing course I did at Columbia Business School, NY, in 2021, who also happens to be the author of the highly recommended bestseller *The Digital Transformation Roadmap.*

Ads only play the role of creating awareness and curiosity. For everything else—such as driving brand likability, preference, purchase, and advocacy—it is brand reputation that influences consumer decisions.

Consumer Curiosity Beyond FOP (Front Of Pack)

CHAPTER XXXVI

Customer Centricity To Participation Centricity

This is arguably the most dramatic change to hit brand building and marketing as a domain. Customers have now ceased to be mute receivers of brand communications. Not only that, their say in it has an unmistakable impact on the brand. About 15 years ago, I recall that at the global ad agency I worked at, we included a slick video in our credentials presentation to showcase that we are an organisation that understood how brand communications had moved from a 'one to many' to a 'many to many' system.

The long-term repercussions of this change, however, are a lot clearer to see today. A brand's communications journey is no longer executed by the business owners and employees alone. No matter how carefully we curate it, it is being shaped by the audience, in equal measure. This would have been fine if we could have formally inducted every current, potential, and tentative customer there is, into the brand's intended ethos, guidelines, and playbook, the way we do with employees. But alas, that's not how customers roll. Instead of imbibing the brand's stated vision, mission, purpose, personality, and tonality stated in a book, they go with the vibes they get from the product/service and the brand. There is renewed pressure on brands to put their money where their mouth is. In other words, to create opportunities to demonstrate our brand essence in practice.

"If our brand does not live out all that it states in its ads and brand literature through its product, actions, and proactive initiatives, the audience is very likely to write a very different brand book about our brand from the one we strategically and creatively craft."

Brand building has not become difficult, it has just become drastically different. This has put veterans and freshers on a level field, back to the drawing board. For centuries, the name of the game was 'consumer understanding'.

"Today, consumer understanding is incomplete without 'consumer-community understanding'."

It would be a mistake to have this sort of approach only in digital marketing and not when creating mass videos for TV-style ads, if that is still a thing. The video ad or the TV ad, if you please, is but a cog in the same wheel. Even offline touchpoints are never disconnected from the digital. Be it under a bus stop, on an escalator at the mall, in a physical store, or while handling the physical product, we know that people are accessing us online, at all times.

"Not approaching every offline touchpoint as a phygital touchpoint compromises impact."

Our brand wheels and brand keys pivot around TG description and a TG insight/tension point that our brand states to be the solution provider for. Perhaps in the reinvented wheel, we need to start with stating the *'TG participation insight'*. An endeavour to capture insights on what makes our TG participate and contribute positively to the brand story. This sort of thinking may make us considerate towards the online audience, which arguably, is all of our audience today.

Good companies and good brands always have a fan following, rooting for them. Traditionally, there was little we could do to access and leverage our fans. Today, we have the facility of finding them, engaging with them, and making them feel a sense of ownership of the brand.

Behavioural sciences have revealed that people value things that they psychologically feel are created by them or with their contribution. The loved brands of the future will be the ones built on strategies that leverage the role of 'consumer participation' in them.

Every Cook Loves His/Her/Their Broth

CHAPTER XXXVII

Attention-Grabbing To Attention-Worthy

Why are attention spans diminishing? If you say, *"too many distractions,"* well, you are right. But, why do we allow ourselves to be distracted? Probably because we don't even know that we have just been distracted in the moment that we have shifted focus. In fact, we believe that we are multi-focusing and not really shifting it. Like when we check our phone even if it's in the middle of a meeting. While we are talking. We pause momentarily, get completely derailed before we apologise and get back to the point. But, we think that we have successfully multi-focused. The same happens when watching a thrilling plot twist in a riveting OTT series. We think we can effortlessly scroll through industry news highlights at the same time. Soon after, we are faced with having to decide whether to rewind or just guess what happened based on what's currently going on in the story.

One of the biggest problems we face, at any given moment of awake and asleep time, is distractions. For which we have devised several solutions. There are apps that help us block distracting apps for desired durations of time. Some of us practice digital detox where we go off the grid entirely for a few days or longer. Announced or unannounced for some drama. We discipline ourselves into strict sleep routine regimes as per psychiatric prescriptions with or without the aid of medicines. The problem persists and our efforts to solve the problem continue.

A culture where it is considered a virtue to actively work towards *not* paying attention to everything puts marketers in quite the conundrum. Unsurprisingly, the brainstorms in marketing and advertising agencies continue to be aimed at fighting for audience attention. But what if we stopped fighting and started to ride the wave instead? It's what prevents us from drowning in the ocean. Should work here too.

The wave we need to ride is that of the reality that people are stuck in lifestyles which demand doing multiple things at once at all times.

> *"We are in an endless rut of knocking off priorities, secondary priorities and a host of other important tasks and things we can't classify as important but really, really want to do."*

It may be foolhardy and definitely uncaring to expect people to stop everything to pay attention to our brand message. The answer then, is to meet them mid-way and not demand their full captive attention. Let them still be driving, cleaning, exercising, falling asleep, cooking or designing while they receive our messaging.

> *"The more our message can be multitasked with, the greater the willingness or sheer ability to pay some attention to us."*

Of course, the task doesn't end there. Every area of focus in this arena is being evaluated for whether it should or should not be replaced by multiple others waiting in line or rather, in an unruly crowd. This takes the need for consumer-centricity to newer levels of sophistication. There is very little room for force-fit seller/manufacturers-speak.

"Brand messages have to constantly provide value, even when it's audio with a higher chance of attention retention, to be able to have people stick on, return and engage with us."

If there's one of the five senses that absolutely can't multitask, it is 'seeing'. But hey! hearing can. At any given point we are adept at processing several sounds around us. Perhaps this explains why audiobooks are popular today. As are podcasts. Somehow, the duration time of the content is not a deterrent when it comes to these mediums. There is merit in leveraging audio as much as possible in the media mix. Or folding-in audio into the entire media mix. This means providing a QR code next to news articles or advertorials that can be scanned to be able to listen to it while doing something else at the same time.

Today, to be even one of the shimmery balls being juggled is to be on target. What we can aim for is some of their attention and then retain it by ensuring they immediately find us 'attention-worthy'. For that we need to provide value. A few non-brainers include content around how to stop wasting time, how to make better decisions, how to eliminate stress, how to balance work and family, how to improve sleep. No matter the industry, all brands need to do is cater to the universal need for self-care/self-improvement/stress relief in a mindlessly multi-tasked world.

Multi-Focussing

CHAPTER XXXVIII

Advertising And Ready Assistance

The advent of digital technologies has made the return on investment (ROI) of nearly every element of the advertising and marketing ecosystem measurable. This is arguably the key culprit for the shuffled roles of various elements of the marketing mix. Performance marketing rose to the spotlight overnight for its ability to produce real-time evidence of returns in addition to the facility for real-time iteration to optimise resources. Social media channels, by virtue of already being within the digital ecosystem, were able to improvise and deliver without a protest.

Change is hardest to process for the ones at a clear advantage in the existing system. Trouble only brewed in traditional mass advertising channels. Mass advertising companies were/are not quite ready to let go of the glory of being the channel that set the tone of the show, which every other channel pretty much played along to. Back then, the most impactful medium was television. This, despite the fact that there was no precise way of isolating the impact of a brand campaign run on TV from the impact of point-of-sale (POS) material and on-ground events, pricing, promotions and distribution, etc. TVC (Television Commercial) makers shared the credit when business goals were met but also the blame when business goals were unmet.

In an ad-avoidant world where mass advertising is in a lost battle against a skip-happy audience, the onus of mass advertising returns to what was probably the earliest form of mass advertising: hoardings. The relevance of outdoors as a medium, unlike other mass mediums, remains strong. Today, OOH (out of home) advertising offers marketers a combination of the traditional benefits of the real world and new-age benefits of technology. This opens an exciting new world of possibilities to connect and engage with customers when they are outdoors, with the added bonus of measurability and accountability by combining it with technologies such as QR codes to enable engagement.

The future of any industry today is being driven by digital transformation and innovations to suit the new ecosystem. The advertising and marketing domain, too, is being empowered with the facility to make available a brand, product, or service to the precise audience that is seeking them when they seek them in whatever form it is being sought.

Strategic thinking now has become about how to analyse data to cater to the needs of those customers who are seeking assistance from us or someone like us at any given moment in real-time. Every CTA (call to action) opportunity is also the POP (point of purchase). If the ad is offline, people can order it on their mobile phone at the moment they see it.

> "When we take into cognisance these realities, we will **see** that audience insight mining needs to go beyond identifying a tension point to identifying when, where, and in what ways they will need us. Not just what we sell, but help with research, resolving confusions, and to assure them that they can count on us."

The role of marketing is steadily moving from 'persuasion' to 'ready assistance when ready to make a choice.'

> *"Digitisation not only helps us in measuring ROI but also in being more 'audience-aware' in our strategies."*

Consequently, allowing for hyper-personalised advertising. Ads are being consumed by individuals rather than as a couple, a family, or as a group. Each of us is being addressed through multiple channels based on our individual movements online. This is fuelled by the customer expectation to be able to access brands on the go, in helpful and relevant ways.

> *This spells out exciting times ahead where analytic brains need to hone their creative, innovative faculties and the creative brains need to hone their analytic faculties. The future demands data and tech-informed creativity and innovation with precisely measurable results.*

Advertising Without Ready Assistance Defies Its
Purpose

CHAPTER XXXIX

Community, Change and Brands

While attending Praxis 2024, the world's largest festival of reputation management professionals, I was particularly moved by something Brenda Darden Wilkerson, President and CEO, AnitaB.org, said during her talk: *"Community is one of the greatest tools we have today to address pressing social needs and bring progressive, positive change."* It made me realise that if asked to pick the most transformative gift the internet has given humanity, I would say it is the power to easily create and grow communities.

Not that communities did not exist before. The internet made it massively more convenient to not just start a community of like-minded individuals spanning larger geographies but also to scale it up worldwide and communicate every second of every hour simultaneously with everyone.

> *"This facility in the hands of the general public continues to make governments, policymakers, benefactors of an unjust status quo, and many giant brands tremble."*

The power of community has helped both the public and the brands looking to connect better with the public. In the past decade alone, we have seen the acceleration of positive change. No matter what our situation is, there is a community online waiting for you to join, share, and receive help. Communities are nudging the change they want to see.

It took a hashtag for the #MeToo movement that started in 2014 to bring together nearly every woman in the world. It continues to gain momentum, even 10 years down the line. The most recent example is the exposé on the double standards in the Kerala Film Industry, thanks to the courage of some women who are speaking up. What is giving these women the strength today, more than ever before? The same thing that is giving all their supporters the platform to come forward in alarmingly large numbers. It is community.

WhatsApp has been accused of being a platform for misinformation. But online platforms also actively provide a space for people who want to come together from various crannies of the world to stand against injustice. The #NotInMyName protest is a case in point. From Delhi to Trivandrum, people united by a pressing urge to protest those unnecessary killings in the name of safeguarding religious sentiments stepped out of their homes - at the same time - to mark their opposing stand. In a similar vein, while the roots of the gay rights movement date back to the 1900s, the LGBTQA Pride initiative has taken new wings since the advent of community building on the internet.

> *"The majority of brand custodians around the world still fail to recognise the power of community."*

I have had millennial colleagues, just two years ago, argue that the brand and category we are ideating on did not have the legacy of, say, a Harley-Davidson to garner a community.

*"We need to **see** that we no longer need to wait for a 'cult' following to mobilise and engage with our audience as a community."*

With the facility to interact with our favourite brands and fellow fans directly, a brand that has no online following or fan engagement is considered 'sus', to use Gen Z slang. It's short for suspicious and means shady.

In the realm of social media marketing, community management is a job description but is seldom given due importance by mainstream advertising strategists and brand custodians. Often relegated to some person in a very separate social media agency, classic marketing approaches have us stuck on focusing on celebrity advocacy or the next best thing: identifying YouTube star influencers to amplify our brand message. This amounts to a refusal to actually see what has changed. It amounts to a resistance to change.

Identifying or creating influencers to place brand mentions is one element of the media mix. In addition to that, we need to also allocate equal, if not more, energies to community engagement. We are fast moving to a world of informed, enabled customers where celebrity advocacy doesn't quite cut it like reviews of online peers, unboxing videos, how-to's, ingredient lists, where it was made, company intent, and as much more information as possible.

Brand-building strategy needs to include ways of engaging meaningfully with the people who mention us in a positive way as much as, if not more than, on identifying influencers to plant desired brand messages.

"The future is community. You can't fool a community. Not as easily as fooling an individual,

at least."

Communities are glued together through their common interests and anxieties. A key task would be to identify the value our brand can offer for the causes and concerns that drive our target audience to form these communities.

As communities for change gain momentum, the room for manipulation and loopholes in marketing and advertising diminishes. In order to stay relevant and loved, brands also need to learn to truthfully stand for whatever they claim and also to recognise their followers as communities or activists in their own right.

We need to re-articulate the brand's role in the lives of a people empowered enough to restructure the world through the power of self-formed communities.

Every Desired Consumer Is A Part Of Communities That Represent *Their* Desires

163

A WARM HUG

CHAPTER XL

Some Things Stay The Same

If you have attended a 10-, 20-, or longer-year school reunion, you would probably have found that the more things change, the more things stay the same. Different things, of course. Thirty-nine chapters dedicated to all that has, is, and will change warrant a chapter on the things that will stay the same.

The child in us: An inability to adapt to technology may make some of us feel old, but deep down, everyone has a child in them. A harmless but hilarious prank, the sound of innocent laughter, the wonder of a rainbow, and sometimes even just an aeroplane in the sky; the urge to hop when we see those familiar hopscotch squares chalked on the side of the road and cartoon doodles in a book—these are a few of the things that will always make us smile.

Instinct: Machines may learn enough to mimic emotions, but it will be hard to emulate the human gut. Instinct is something that will set us apart. Always.

Human inspiration: Perseverance, determination, recovering stronger, revolting, leading positive change, empathy, kindness, and a disarming sense of humour—these strengths demonstrated by humans will always inspire.

Human shortcomings: Self-doubt, envy, shattered dreams, disappointments, mental and physical vulnerabilities, feeling bullied or alternatively over-confident, self-centeredness, insatiable restlessness, defending judgmentalism and insensitive jokes, thriving on bullying. The trials, tribulations, and triumphs surrounding these unchanging human traits will always keep the drama alive.

Generation gap: The youngest generation will always face some conflict with the older generation, sometimes even just 10 years older. The race to stay relevant with the passage of time will always remain a challenge for those growing older—a challenge that can be overcome with a little bit of openness.

Resistance to change: It is normal. We just need to be vigilant of it. Just as learning a good habit and getting rid of a bad one takes conscious intent and action, tackling resistance to change takes intent. Commitment is key. The rest will follow.

A warm hug: No matter how much we learn to utilise the convenience and efficiency of a digitised world, we will always want physical, offline human interactions. The good thing is that we have the option of dialling it up or down as per our mood. But the power of a reassuring hug from someone we care about will stay the same. Always.

You've got this!

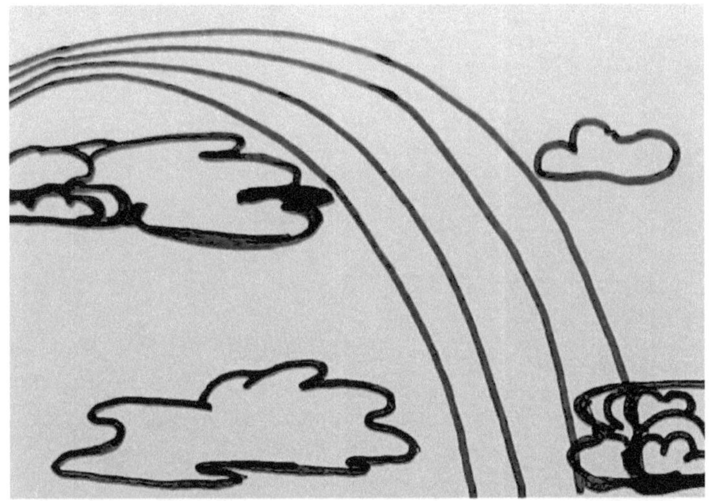

The Joy Of A Rainbow - Even Just A Doodle Of It

About The Author

Pooja's nuanced POV (Point of View) on the business of brand building and marketing strategies comes from over 20 years of versatile practice across leading global giants like Ogilvy, MullenLowe Lintas, Publicis India Advertising, and TBWA at their Mumbai offices. She also had a stint at Saatchi & Saatchi in Colombo, Sri Lanka.

In 2021, she chose Columbia Business School, NYC, to earn her certificate in Digital Marketing. It was a great decision, as it is possibly the only course in the world with a focus on building brands in online marketing and emphasises the inevitability and importance of digital transformation.

She is open about her struggles with MDD (Major Depressive Disorder), first diagnosed in 2022. Can't say if this has anything to do with it, but she is yet to find an agency or consultancy that is ready to offer unified brand strategy across channels, covering both traditional and new-age methods seamlessly. Until then, she offers her services to those who see the need for this independently, as a freelancer. The chapters she finds most pertinent in this book are 'Every Person a Brand' and 'Everyone a Techie.'

Pooja also has the additional distinction of being an ex-actress (you can spot her in the 2015 Bollywood blockbuster Airlift). She is currently a watercolour artist, plays the ukulele, and trains in dance and vocals at her own studio in Indiranagar, Bangalore. She has her mind set on doing more clay sculpting and couverture chocolate making at home. Find her on Instagram @yet_another_pooja and @madness_meet_method.